PROFESSIONALISM IN LOCAL GOVERNMENT

John Nalbandian

MO

PROFESSIONALISM IN LOCAL GOVERNMENT

Transformations in the
Roles, Responsibilities,
and Values of City Managers

Jossey-Bass Publishers

San Francisco • Oxford • 1991

9/0001675

PROFESSIONALISM IN LOCAL GOVERNMENT
Transformations in the Roles, Responsibilities, and Values of City Managers
  by John Nalbandian

Copyright © 1991 by: Jossey-Bass Inc., Publishers
                      350 Sansome Street
                      San Francisco, California 94104

                      &

                      Jossey-Bass Limited
                      Headington Hill Hall
                      Oxford OX3 0BW

Library of Congress Cataloging-in-Publication Data

Nalbandian, John, date.
    Professionalism in local government: transformations in the
  roles, responsibilities, and values of city managers / John
  Nalbandian. — 1st ed.
      p.   cm.—(The Jossey-Bass public administration series)
    Includes bibliographical references and index.
    ISBN 1-55542-372-8
    1. City managers—United States—History. 2. Municipal government
  by city manager—United States—History. I. Title. II. Series.
  JS344.C5N28   1991
  352'.00724'0973—dc 20   91-9408
                                                             CIP

Manufactured in the United States of America

JACKET DESIGN BY WILLI BAUM

FIRST EDITION

Code 9163

The Jossey-Bass
Public Administration Series

Contents

Preface   xi

The Author   xix

**Part One: The Evolution
of Local Government Design**   1

1. The Original Ideal of Council-Manager Government   3

2. Challenges to the Council-Manager Ideal   19

3. Adaptive Responses in Local Government Design   36

**Part Two: Building a Contemporary Foundation
for Professionalism**   49

4. Understanding the Contemporary Role of
    the City Manager   51

5. Accountability: Broadening the Contemporary
    City Manager's Base of Legitimacy   69

6. The Value Base of Contemporary Professionalism   85

7. The Future of Professionalism in Local Government   103

References   109

Index   123

Preface

This book is about local government and the professionals whose craft has changed over the seventy-five-year history of council-manager government. It is about both the idealism that shaped the beginnings of council-manager government and how this form has pragmatically adapted to political challenges. Similarly, the book addresses the roles, responsibilities, and values of city managers—how they have evolved and how they are reflected in a set of contemporary professional tenets.

The book's central thesis is that while structure and practice in council-manager government have adapted realistically to the changing political, economic, and social forces in modern communities, the philosophical foundation for professionalism in local government has not kept pace. There remains an orthodox view of city management that is at odds with contemporary practice. Consequently, the profession struggles intermittently to find its place in the modern context of democratic governance (Bollens and Ries, 1969; Stillman 1974). This gap between what managers actually do and the orthodox view distances them from normative guidance about their roles and responsibilities and also about the values that underpin the decisions they make. Further, this gap creates a barrier to citizens—the ultimate source of legitimacy in governance—who might otherwise better understand professionalism in government. This book seeks to close the gap by deriving the tenets of contemporary professionalism in city management from professional practice and placing them firmly within the context of democratic governance.

My interest in the local government professional relates directly to my experiences over the last fifteen years at the University of Kansas. Only after arriving in Lawrence did I begin to appreciate the long-standing connection between city management and the university. Lawrence housed the first permanent secretariat for the International City Management Association (ICMA); Orin Nolting, the third executive director of the ICMA, was a political science graduate of the University of Kansas; in 1948 professors Ethan Allen and Edwin Stene established a graduate program in public administration with the express purpose of training people to become city managers; as of the late 1980s some 20 percent of the annual awards given by the ICMA had gone to University of Kansas graduates; from 1977 to 1987 four of ten ICMA elected presidents were KU alumni; and at one time in the mid-1980s the chief administrative officers in Dallas, Fort Worth, San Antonio, Wichita, the District of Columbia, Mecklenberg County (Charlotte), and Montgomery County (Dayton) were all KU graduates. It is hard for a faculty member to avoid city management with that kind of history, as well as frequent reminders from a vigilant alumni.

During my tenure at Kansas University, especially from 1983 to 1988 as chair of the Department of Public Administration, it seemed as if my contact with city management professionals was nearly as frequent as my contact with students. I began to sense an uneasiness about the profession of city management from those who practice it. Managers would talk openly among themselves about their policy-making responsibilities and the fact that political and economic situations in their communities required them to coordinate, broker, and negotiate community interests more than ever. In contrast, to lay audiences or in newspapers, articles, brochures, or short films that introduced council-manager government, these same managers, and other advocates of council-manager government, would describe the official work of city managers differently. In these encapsulated descriptions managers were portrayed as less politically involved, more the implementers of public policy and less the brokers and negotiators of community interests. They were the managers of the city's internal operations rather than community leaders.

In short, "officially" the city manager is described as a policy implementer who is responsive to the governing body and brings to the foreground the value of efficiency in government operations. The practical world of city management often suggests a more complicated view. The manager is deeply involved in policy-making as well as implementation, responds to a multitude of community forces as well as to the governing body, and incorporates a variety of competing values into the decision-making process.

This difference between the practice of city management and the way that practice was described to uninitiated audiences captured my interest, and I started to think about a book that would bring together "theory-in-practice" and "espoused theory." At first, I thought something must be wrong with the practice because the espoused theory connected so nicely with the tenets of democracy and seemed so simple to grasp. Then I realized that the situation was much more complex; the practice worked, tempered by a largely unspoken appreciation of democratic values. But practice threatened the espoused theory, which had been built into an orthodoxy based on the intellectual notion that politics was the distinct realm of the elected official and the city manager was limited to administration. Even though outdated and severely challenged since the end of World War II, the espoused theory remains intellectually attractive today because it creates the image that elected officials control local government professionals.

My thoughts on the needed realignment between theory-in-practice and espoused theory shifted. Rather than prescribe new practices to fit the ideal, I wanted to crystallize and articulate a revised ideal in the form of tenets of professionalism. My primary goal was to derive these tenets from practice and to formulate them in a way that would place city management firmly in the context of contemporary democratic governance. This is what I try to accomplish in the following chapters.

The goal of articulating an espoused theory of city management is confounded by the dual role that a theory of a public service profession must fulfill. On the one hand, espoused theory should include propositions that describe what the public service professional actually does. On the other hand, the theory must place the profession firmly within the principles and context of democratic governance. The accomplishment of both tasks becomes a norma-

tive guide for practice. Thus, an espoused theory of city management must describe what professionalism "is" and what it "ought
to be." Theory provides the crucial link between practice and
principle.

One of my purposes in writing this book is to give a voice
to city management professionals. They practice democracy every
day by delivering public services to citizens in their communities
and in their own way elaborate upon the meaning of democracy in
action. By listening to them, I have learned about democracy as well
as city management.

Additional sources included scholarly literature, as well as
newspaper reports from small and large cities that provide a real-
life and timely perspective on council-manager government. I have
made extensive use of the words of local government professionals
as given in a series of interviews (Nalbandian and Davis, 1987).
While many of these professionals have changed positions since the
interviews, I have identified them with the positions they held at the
time of the interviews in order to provide an accurate context for
their remarks.

Audience

Professionalism in Local Government is for local government professionals who are willing to reflect upon their profession and their
work. Because the book describes contemporary professionalism,
those who read it will probably measure their own practice against
what their contemporaries have said and what I have written. I hope
that new insights will emerge from this reflection to inform the
individual local government professional's work.

Students, our future local government professionals, will
find in the book managers struggling with the same kinds of questions they eventually will face themselves. Hopefully, this preview
will help them prepare for the self-reflection they can anticipate.

Underlying this book is the assumption that professional
practice is enhanced with insight into one's profession and where
it fits in the broader scheme of government and public service. This
is not a book about economic development, neighborhood politics,
infrastructure repair, or the nuts and bolts of service delivery. The

book is for those who want to know more about how council-manager government began and the ideals that spawned it, as well as how the structure of council-manager government and the roles, responsibilities, and values of city managers have been transformed.

Overview of the Contents

Part One addresses the origins, design, criticisms, and adaptations that have taken place in the structure of council-manager government. Part Two discusses the way the roles, responsibilities, and values of city management have changed and describes the tenets of professionalism that have evolved.

Chapter One looks at the origins of the council-manager plan in the context of government reform at the turn of the century. I have two goals in this chapter. First, I want to give the reader a sense of the ideals of council-manager government and professionalism in city management as they were envisioned at the time of adoption. It is my belief that fundamental parts of these ideals remain in the orthodox, yet dated, view of city management. Second, I want readers to see the problems of government that the council-manager plan was supposed to solve and what new ones it inadvertently invited. Many contemporary attacks on city managers and council-manager government stem from criticisms that are inherent in the design of council-manager government, not in the way it is practiced.

Chapter Two examines contemporary pressures and tensions in the council-manager plan. These include claims by some politicians, civil rights advocates, community activists, newspaper editorialists, and citizen critics that professionals exert too much power, that minority views are underrepresented, and that council-manager government hinders development of political leadership and political accountability to citizens.

The criticisms outlined in Chapter Two have stimulated numerous transformations in the structure of council-manager government. Chapter Three details these changes, which include the way the governing body is elected, the power and role of the mayor, and mechanisms that require less reliance of council members on professional staff for information.

The first three chapters describe changes in structure and

argue that they strengthen the foundation of council-manager government by aligning it with contemporary political values. The remaining chapters make a slightly different point. Although the roles, responsibilities, and values of city managers have adapted to contemporary urban environments, to strengthen council-manager government the changes must be placed intellectually within the context of democratic governance. The last four chapters describe the changes and attempt to meet the intellectual challenge by formulating tenets of contemporary professionalism that are derived from practice and situated in representative democracy.

Chapter Four outlines the contemporary role of the city manager following the suggestions by Svara (1985, 1990; also Boynton and Wright, 1971; Wikstrom, 1979) that governance under the council-manager plan should be viewed as a shared responsibility between elected officials and local government professionals. The manager is actively involved in brokering and negotiating community interests, and council members actively and politically participate in what formerly were viewed as areas of exclusive staff domain.

The partnership concept of governance blurs lines of responsibility and invites examination of the perennial question that connects democracy and public service: How is political control to be maintained over nonelected professional staff? This question is addressed in Chapter Five, where it is argued that informal mechanisms of accountability have arisen over the years to supplement the governing body's formal responsibility for political oversight. Managers have accepted responsibility to become aware of and responsive to community values as expressed by groups and citizens in addition to the governing body. This responsiveness to community values broadens the base of legitimacy for the transformation that has taken place in the manager's role. As governing bodies have shared their political responsibilities with managers, managers have begun to seek political anchors for their expanded role.

While Chapter Five argues that managers are looking to a broad array of community values to legitimize their role, Chapter Six identifies representativeness, individual rights, and social equity, in addition to efficiency, as values that have come to underpin the practice of city management. The chapter focuses on how these values have influenced administrative processes and decision making in contemporary city management.

Chapter Seven speculates on the importance of building professionalism on a base of values rather than on the structural characteristics of council-manager government. It goes on to suggest that the politics and administration dichotomy, which has failed to describe what managers actually do, nevertheless continues to stimulate debate regarding how to bring expert knowledge to bear on public policy-making while retaining the supremacy of political values. This recurring question's importance to those concerned with democratic theory ensures periodic interest in the roles, responsibilities, and values of local government professionals.

Acknowledgments

Over the years, I have had the wonderful opportunity to become acquainted with a number of very thoughtful and dedicated local government professionals. Many of these people have shared their work with me while others have read and commented upon various chapters of the book. I have tried to write about their world, and I could not have completed this project without their help.

Professionalism in Local Government is better for the critiques provided by the publisher's reviewers. I have not always agreed with their comments, nor have I always been encouraged by them, but in the end their reviews have proven valuable. My colleagues in the Department of Public Administration have encouraged me throughout. We share a norm of productivity and have developed a climate of support and civility, and I could ask no more of them.

Most important, I want to thank Carol and John, my wife and son. Often we go our independent ways comforted by the warmth and security of our home base. And finally, I want to thank my friend Gary Cox, who has stayed with me through the best and most difficult times.

Lawrence, Kansas   John Nalbandian
June 1991

To all the Nalbandians and Kehayans—
for their love of family
and respect for community

The Author

John Nalbandian is professor in the Department of Public Administration at the University of Kansas. He received his B.A. (1965) and M.A. (1967) degrees in international relations and his Ph.D. (1977) in public administration, all from the University of Southern California.

Nalbandian's main research interests lie in the fields of human resources management and the relationship between democracy and professionalism in local government. He received the International City Management Association's Stephen B. Sweeney award as Local Government Educator of the Year in 1988 and was recognized as Academic Administrator of the Year in 1988 by the Greater Kansas City Chapter of the American Society for Public Administration. He is coauthor (with D. Klingner) of *Public Personnel Management: Contexts and Strategies* (1985) and (with R. G. Davis) of *Reflections of Local Government Professionals* (1987).

Nalbandian served as Chair of the Department of Public Administration from 1983 to 1988. He has been invited to speak to city management associations in five states and on two occasions to the International City Management Association's annual meeting. He has served as consultant or trainer to local governments and other public management groups on over seventy-five occasions. In 1991 he was elected to a four-year term as a city commissioner in Lawrence, Kansas.

PROFESSIONALISM IN LOCAL GOVERNMENT

Part One

THE EVOLUTION OF LOCAL GOVERNMENT DESIGN

1

The Original Ideal
of Council-Manager Government

The structure of council-manager government and the roles, responsibilities, and values of city managers have changed over the past seventy-five years, and yet an orthodox view of city management has remained largely intact. This divergence distances city management professionals from the guidance that an updated, realistic theory of city management could provide, and it creates difficulties when city managers try to describe their work to citizens and elected officials unfamiliar with council-manager government. In order to understand the differences between the traditional view and modern practice, it is necessary to revisit the first several decades of this century when the orthodox view developed. I will review the origins of city management with particular attention to the orthodox view that emerged (Price, 1941; Stillman, 1977). Stillman (1974) and Svara (1989c, 1989d) have prepared more comprehensive chronological histories that I have not attempted to duplicate.

According to Stillman (1977), the traditional view is woven around the symbols that advocates adopted in order to promote council-manager government and the concept of a city manager. These symbols—the idea that politics and administration were separate spheres of activity, the political neutrality of the city manager,

3

and the virtuous nature of expertise and efficiency—developed over several decades of reform and administrative theory.

On two occasions, Stillman (1974, 1977), a highly regarded scholar of city management, has acknowledged the importance of the symbols for contemporary city management. According to Stillman (1977), the symbols have influenced the structure of council-manager government as well as the role of the city manager, and they have given rise to "fundamental value problems associated with this line of work" (p. 660).

The symbols of any movement will diverge in some measure from the practices they represent and eventually may assume a life of their own. This observation is appropriate when discussing the city manager, who is described by the orthodox view as a politically neutral administrative expert. In fact, Svara (1989c, 1989d) has shown convincingly that the line between politics and administration has always been blurred and that city managers have always been involved in policy formulation. Beginning with White (1927) and Stone, Price, and Stone (1940), an overwhelming number of academic studies have shown the same.

Yet the persistent attention the orthodox view claims is seen in the challenges it invites many years after these early studies appeared. For example, in 1958 Bosworth felt compelled to write an article entitled "The Manager *Is* a Politician" [his emphasis]. In 1964 Bromage wrote: "City managers are no longer viewed as administrative caretakers unconcerned with the actions of the council and neutral to policy. Managers are drawn into policy making, politics if you prefer, by recommending goals and programs to council" (p. 1). In 1977 Stillman entitled a piece on city managers "The City Manager: Professional Helping Hand, or Political Hired Hand?" And in 1988 Ammons and Newell wrote an article bearing the title " 'City Managers Don't Make Policy': A Lie; Let's Face It."

As another example of the power of the orthodox view of city management, a respected city manager, active in the International City Management Association (ICMA) and a member of that group's Future Horizons Project, describes his present job as administrator of a large, dynamic metropolitan county in the following way on his brief résumé: "The County Administrator is responsible for *implementing policies* adopted by the Board of County Commissioners and managing subordinates in the *execution of Commission directives*. The County Administrator maintains liaison with elected officials and independent County Boards, coordinates delivery of services by 1600 employees, directs the development and administration of the annual operational and capital budgets totaling $100 million, and *makes recommendations on program options* to the Board of County Commissioners" (emphasis added).

To summarize this point, despite convincing evidence to the contrary, the city manager's actual role is still measured against the traditional view that symbolizes the manager as a politically neutral, administrative expert who serves at the pleasure of a governing body. How can an image like this prevail despite the contrary evidence that both academician and manager accept? First, the symbol does describe some part of the city manager's practice. It is not totally disconnected and, therefore, cannot be disregarded. Second, and perhaps more important, the political supremacy denoted in the symbol of the politically neutral administrator places the role of the city manager firmly within the context of representative democracy. It does so elegantly and completely, even if not accurately.

The orthodox view that I will describe in this chapter paints a simple, comprehensive, and internally logical picture of city management and places it within the context of representative democracy. It is short on accuracy, but it answers a very sticky and enduring normative question about government in America: How can we govern democratically and efficiently?

There are three propositions that I suggest constitute the foundations of an orthodox view of city management:

1. The work of city managers *isolates* them from partisan politics and often from community politics and policy-making as well;
2. The city manager is a *politically neutral* administrative expert accountable to a representative governing body.
3. *Efficiency* and political responsiveness can be harmoniously pursued in the community.

The Politics and Administration Dichotomy

Reform in local government at the turn of the century operated against a political backdrop unfamiliar to managers in most contemporary communities. The presence of legislative and executive branches of government was common, bicameral legislatures existed, numerous administrative as well as political officials were elected, and partisan politics were the norm. The watchword for the design of governmental form was vigilance against the arrogation of power—the spirit in which the United States Constitution was born.

Efficiency suffered under these various forms of local government, which were built on the ideas of checks and balances and separation of legislative and executive powers. In 1923 Crane, having assembled a digest of 166 council-manager charters, commented on the separation of powers as a design principle: "The doctrine of the separation of powers or of checks and balances as it is alternatively called, is designed as a protection to individual liberty against the possibility of government tyranny. As such it may have its place in the nation and in the states. With the safeguards of national and state law thrown about the rights of person and property, however, *there can be no danger of tyranny by a local government, from which the only real dangers are extravagance and inefficiency*" (1923, Section Two, p. 1, emphasis added).

These inefficiencies resulted from machine politics and political spoils. Political machines were, in part, vehicles allowing common citizens—a large number of them immigrants—to make their way through the governmental mazes of the time. In addition, they provided a way for the legislature to coordinate or control the discretion of independently elected members of the executive branch (Goodnow, [1900] 1967).

In order to perpetuate themselves, political machines relied in part on personnel appointments through systems of "spoils" and through favoritism in the award of governmental contracts, franchises, purchasing, and licenses. In short, what we regard today as administrative processes subject to the norms of impartiality and efficiency were vehicles of self-interest and the currency of political exchange. To the reformer, government had become corrupt. People sought office for self-interest, and inefficiency was common.

One way the reformers responded to corruption and inefficiency was by seeking to remove politics from administrative processes and reducing administration to a technical field subject to rational analysis and management principles rather than political considerations. This view peaked in the 1930s when it grew to dominate what has become an orthodox view of city management (Stillman, 1974; Svara, 1989d).

In 1938, the ICMA revised its original Code of Ethics to include a preamble that contained the following prescriptions about politics and administration: "In order to achieve effective, democratic government, the council-manager plan provides that municipal policy shall be determined exclusively by a legislative body created by the people and that the administration of policy shall be vested in the city manager who, as administrative head of the city, shall be appointed by and responsible to the council" (Stillman, 1974, p. 124).

Scholars trace the politics and administration dichotomy to Woodrow Wilson's work ([1887] 1987), "The Study of Administration," where it served Wilson more as an intellectual tool than an empirical discovery. Wilson observed that managing the day-to-day operations of government had become exceedingly complex, a task frequently beset by inefficiency, graft, and corruption. His familiar words succinctly make the point: "The weightier debates of constitutional principle are even yet by no means concluded; but they are no longer of more immediate practical moment than questions of administration. It is getting to be harder to *run* a constitution than to frame one" (p. 12). Seeking to cleanse and streamline government operations, Wilson confronted a major intellectual puzzle. The administrative models that he admired were featured in the European autocratic monarchies, which Americans scorned. How could he borrow principles of administration from governments whose purposes set them apart?

Wilson asserted that politics and administration were *separate* endeavors and aspects of governance. Moreover, they were arranged hierarchically—as distinguished from the traditional separation of powers where branches of government were equal—with administration the means to political ends. He proposed to borrow the means while rejecting the ends. Again, familiar words make his point: "If I see a murderous fellow sharpening a knife cleverly, I can borrow his way of sharpening the knife without borrowing his probable intention to commit murder with it; and so, if I see a monarchist dyed in the wool managing a public bureau well, I can learn his business methods without changing one of my republican spots" (p. 24).

Wilson's theoretical accomplishment permitted the development and application of administrative expertise, measured by the criteria of economy and efficiency, which could be isolated from the day-to-day interference of politics. Further, it connected administration to politics instrumentally, thus handling elegantly the crucial issue in democratic theory of how to hold appointed officials accountable to democratic principles and control.

Goodnow ([1900] 1967), writing some thirteen years after Wilson's essay appeared, noted that "the action of the state as a political entity consists either in operations necessary to the expression of its will, or in operations necessary to the execution of that will" (p. 9). He continued: "Politics has to do with the policies or expressions of the state will. Administration has to do with the execution of these policies" (p. 18). Some twenty years after council-manager government was introduced, White (1927) wrote: "In general, the charter of city-manager cities assumes a sharp differentiation of legislative (policy-forming) powers, and administrative (policy-executing) powers" (p. 154).

Not only were politics and administration viewed as distinct spheres of action, the essence of city government was seen as falling into the administrative sphere—providing services efficiently (Ridley and Nolting, 1934). Goodnow ([1900] 1967) wrote: "Municipal government is very largely a matter of administration in the narrow sense of the word. This is the truth at the bottom of the claim which is so often made, that municipal government is a matter of business" (p. 84). Twenty-six years later, White (1926) succinctly noted that "the business of government in the twentieth century is fundamentally the business of administration'" (p. 24). White's book, *The City Manager,* was published the following year.

While the concept that politics and administration effectively permitted the development of administrative rationality free of partisan political interference, to this day the dichotomy has endured not as a guide to practice, but as the pin that links the world of administration to the tenets of representative democracy—it is an intellectual device. In discussing the politics and administration dichotomy as recently as 1984, Waldo ([1948] 1984) reiterated in the second edition of the *Administrative State:* "It had become customary to presume that in rejecting the politics-administration dichotomy as a crude fiction, we had solved the problem of a proper relationship between these two realms. But not so. The problems are still there, however, obscured and ignored" (p. xxxiv). In sum, while the politics and administration dichotomy fails to describe accurately the practice of management, it does an eminent job of placing the ideal into the context of representative democracy. It connects these two spheres of action by asserting political supremacy over administrative rationality. With that as its purpose, it constitutes an important part of the orthodox view of city management.

Political Accountability and Administrative Neutrality

While the separation of powers in the federal and most state constitutions divides legislative and administrative functions vertically into coequal branches of government, council-manager government conceptually distinguishes these functions but then unifies legislative and administrative authority in a single, small governing body. It reflects the argument that all power should flow from a small governing body that is easily held accountable through election (Childs, 1913; Childs, Waite, and others, 1916). The executive, who would be responsible for all administrative operations, reports to the governing body, which would restrict itself to questions of public policy.

The primary concern of the reformers was to make government accountable to the people, not to political machines. As Goodnow ([1900] 1967) pointed out, the decentralization of authority in government fed the need for political machines as coordinating mechanisms. Eliminating the large number of elected offices and focusing attention on a small governing body could restore control of government to the people.

The council-manager form of government grew out of what is called the "short ballot movement," headed by Richard Childs (1965). In fact, Childs saw the council-manager form, which he developed, as a vehicle to advance the short ballot. The short-ballot idea aimed to reduce the number of elected offices in a community so that citizens could focus their attention on a few political contests. With so many offices, including judgeships and administrative positions like city treasurer, city attorney, city clerk, and auditor on the ballot, it was easy for slates to be elected and for people to vote for parties rather than concentrate on local issues. In addition, it was difficult to focus political accountability with so many elected offices.

A second concern had to do with administrative accountability, made salient by the proposition that politics and administration were seen as separate spheres of activity. Isolating administrative staff from politics permits expertise to develop, but it raises questions of authoritative political control. To promote efficiency and ensure political control, the reformers sought to consolidate administrative processes under a single executive position (New York State Constitutional Convention Commission, 1915; Ridley and Nolting, 1934) and to hold that executive accountable to a governing body. The executive, of course, was the city manager who would serve at the pleasure of the governing body.

Formally, it was fairly easy to describe the city manager's job. White (1927) observed that "the city manager is primarily an administrative officer" (p. 157). He cites the 1913 charter of the city of Dayton as providing an "admirable statement" of the manager's duties. It is worth repeating here as evidence of the nonpolitical role assumed for the city manager.

1. To see that the laws and ordinances are enforced.
2. To appoint and remove all directors of departments and all subordinate officers . . . subject to operations of the Civil Service Commission.
3. To control all departments and divisions.
4. To investigate the affairs of any department or the conduct of any official or employee.
5. To require the commission to appoint advisory boards.
6. To prepare and submit to the commission a budget.

In contrast to this clearly administrative role, Svara (1989d) shows that discussion of the National Civic League's Model City Charter of 1915, which endorsed council-manager government, clearly envisioned a policy-active role for the manager. For example, "The manager must 'show himself to be a leader, formulating policies and urging their adoption by the council'" (cited in Svara, 1989d, p. 345). Even Childs, who frequently cautioned managers to observe their primary duty to the governing body said, "The great city managers of tomorrow will be those whose ideal stopped at no line of dogma or tradition but who pushed beyond old horizons and discovered new worlds of service" (cited in White, 1927, pp. 188–189).

According to White (1927), the role of the city manager was subject to controversy even in the earliest discussions among city managers. He noted that there were two schools of thought: "One school of thought insists that the manager 'is the servant absolutely of the commission,' that a clear demarcation can and should be made between the legislative and administrative functions of a city government, that the manager should devote himself exclusively to the latter. . . . The opposing school of thought denies that a clear demarcation can be made between the duties of the manager and the council; points out that the manager is necessarily the center of public interest, that he cannot shelter himself behind the council; and inquires whether after all the manager must not inevitably become a community-leader, dealing with council and people on a broad base of policy and program as well as the the narrower base of city administration" (p. 183).

What does seem clear among these differences is a consensus that the manager should not be involved in partisan politics, political campaigns, or even party demonstrations (White, 1927). Almost as clear is the requirement for *neutrality* in political controversy (Stone, Price, and Stone, 1940), frequently extending to avoidance of controversial public policy recommendations.

Over a short period of time, the concept of neutrality, defined as avoiding political controversy, seemed to expand and narrow the policy-related role envisioned for the manager. For example, in 1934, Ridley and Nolting, the executive director and assistant director of the International City Managers' Association wrote: "For a manager to take the lead in policy results in making the manager's position a political office, thus sacrificing confidence in his professional outlook and greatly limiting his usefulness as an executive" (p. 38).

Changes in the City Manager's Code of Ethics, developed in 1924 and revised in 1938, reinforced this trend toward neutrality. In 1924, Article 12 implied a behind-the-scenes role for the manager in community politics by stating, "No City Manager should take an *active* (emphasis added) part in politics." Article 5 implied a role for the manager in policy formulation by stating, "Loyalty to his employment recognizes that it is the council, the elected representative of the people, who *primarily* (emphasis added) determine the municipal policies, and are entitled to the credit for their fulfillment." In 1938 the association eliminated the ambiguity in the political role and seemed at least to hold to the status quo, if not limit the policy role somewhat, stating: "The city manager is in no sense a political leader. In order that policy may be intelligent and effective, he provides the council with information and advice, but he encourages positive decisions on policy by the council instead of passive acceptance of his recommendations." These revisions, limiting the political/policy role, take place paradoxically at a time when Stone, Price, and Stone (1940) clearly recognize that "to ask a city manager to avoid incursion into policy would be to set up an impossible distinction between policy and administration; it would be, in effect, to ask him not to be a city manager" (p. 247).

Along the lines suggested earlier by Price (1941) and Stillman (1977), Svara (1989d) comments on this apparent contrast between public pronouncements about council-manager government and the reality that Stone, Price and Stone (1940) and White (1927) had observed in their analyses of city manager government. Svara observes: "Perhaps to allay suspicions that council-manager government would lead to administrative dominance, publicists of the plan went even further and reinforced the idea that the manager should be simply an administrative technician" (p. 345). Administrative dominance and democratic control conflict. Thus, in order to encourage adoption and support of council-manager government, the manager's role is depoliticized in theory and symbol, if not in fact.

Efficiency and the Public Interest

The idea that the city manager was a politically neutral, administrative expert fit nicely with the scientific management advocate's view of efficiency. The value of efficiency transcended the business world and administrative practice in general. As Waldo (1948) has observed about the period after World War I: "Most interesting from the standpoint of the theoretical literature of public administration was the doubt and self-examination occasioned by German successes, and the resultant emphasis upon 'efficiency' as a necessary element of democracy. The unquestioned faith in democracy as a superior way of life and the boundless confidence in its ultimate triumph were shaken by the smooth precision and smashing power of Germany at war. Voices were raised and hearts were troubled, seeking an answer to the question why the unrighteous should flourish. The answer was 'efficiency.' If democracy were to survive it somehow had to add efficiency to its ideals of liberty and equality. It had to bring efficiency out of factory, school, and home, where it was already a popular ideal, and make the nation as a whole an efficient business" (pp. 10–11).

For the reformers, efficiency opposed corruption. According to Haber (1964), "Efficiency and good came closer to meaning the same thing in these years than in any other period of American history" (p. ix). How could anyone argue against efficiency in government when efficiency was seen as a moral good? Efficiency and the public interest went hand in glove. Efficiency stood for competence, rationality, impartiality, and planning. As Crane (1923) reminded us earlier, the worst sins of municipal government were "extravagance and inefficiency" (Section Two, p. 1).

The global connotation of efficiency gradually narrowed, although its preeminence went unchallenged. Efficiency came to focus more specifically on administration and the internal operations of an organized enterprise. Whereas late nineteenth-century civil service reform had hoped to promote efficiency simply by eliminating politics from administration, gradually the scientific management movement applied engineering thinking and concepts to the understanding and design of work and the role of a manager.

The scientific management movement captured the unbridled faith in science and rationality in the early twentieth century (Waldo, [1948] 1984). Experts could solve the public's problems where municipal politics had failed. White (1926) pointedly asserted: "To what extent the modern state now depends upon science is not easily described, for the whole technical equipment of present day administration rests upon scientific achievement. More than that, the modern administrator has become not only a scientist, but a research scientist" (p. 14). Urwick (1937b) went so far as to characterize Taylor and Fayol, giants of the scientific and administrative management movements of the 1920s and 1930s, as "scientists before they were managers. Both men gave the devotion of their later lives to putting science into management" (p. 118).

In 1927 Willoughby observed: "The position is here taken that, in administration, there are certain fundamental principles of general application analogous to those characterizing any science which must be observed if the end of administration, efficiency in operation, is to be secured" (p. ix).

In 1937 Urwick (1937a) set the tone for a classic collection of essays about administrative theory, with these words: "It is the general thesis of this paper that there are principles which can be arrived at inductively from the study of human experience of organization, which should govern arrangements for human association of any kind. These principles can be studied as a technical question, irrespective of the purpose of the enterprise, the personnel comprising it, or any constitutional, political or social theory underlying its creation" (p. 49).

As the scientific management movement grew in the early part of the century, the belief in scientific analysis and problem solving reached its peak. There was one best way to build sidewalks, sewers, bridges, and streets, and there was little, if any, room for politics in the process. To this day managers say, "There is no Republican or Democratic way to pick up the garbage."

This characterization of the manager as a scientist comports with the view of the manager as a politically neutral, administrative expert and with the realistic observation that numerous city managers were, in fact, trained as engineers. The city manager is viewed as an administrative professional who should be allowed to exercise expertise protected from the vagaries of partisan politics. Theoretically, there simply is no place for politics in science where the goal is truth and the means are rational thought and method. Gulick (1937) implies the distinctive nature of efficiency when he writes about politics and profits: "It does not seem to this writer, however, that these interferences with efficiency in any way eliminate efficiency as the fundamental value upon which the science of administration may be erected. They serve to condition and to complicate, but not to change the single ultimate test of value in administration" (p. 193).

Gulick's essay shows how the term *efficiency* lost some of its "good government" moralism yet retained its value: "The fundamental objective of the science of administration is the accomplishment of work in hand with the least expenditure of man-power and materials. Efficiency is thus axiom number one in the value scale of administration" (p. 192).

According to Stillman (1974), "'Economy and efficiency,' twin values of the business community, frequently found their way into the literature on city managers" (p. 8). In fact, Childs adopted the title "city manager" after the "general manager" common in business enterprise (Stone, Price, and Stone, 1940). According to Stone, Price, and Stone, "Perhaps the most popular argument in favor of the city manager plan was the analogy of the business corporation" (p. 27). If one separated the policy-making function from administrative functions, unified rather than separated power, and then consolidated administrative authority in a chief administrative officer, one could replicate the model of a business organization (Childs, 1913, 1965; Willoughby, 1927).

A review of the proceedings of the national meetings of city managers from 1914 to 1917 shows them to be filled with references to business methods. Virtually every improvement in city government a manager cites at these meetings is related to eliminating politics from administration or bringing administrative order and business methods to municipal operations. In 1916 the managers even established a committee to develop standardized forms that could be used by municipalities nationwide (City Managers' Association, 1916).

Efficiency and Community Harmony

Of the three beliefs held by the reformers and administrative theorists of the 1920s and 1930s, the council-manager plan reflects most clearly their esteem for efficiency. Further, in what Svara (1989d) criticizes as a flawed revisionist view, the council-manager form of government, with its emphasis on expertise and the business corporation, in some ways sought to depoliticize the community—not only from partisan politics but from all politics.

The city manager is seen as the professional, the administrative expert whose knowledge of managerial principles and scientific techniques frame the planning and decisions required to deliver municipal services efficiently and economically. Adherents of scientific management and administrative theory in the 1920s and 1930s focus on the commonalities between organizations rather than the differences between business and government. Organizations as social entities are viewed as machines (Mooney, 1937; Willoughby, 1927). Gulick and Urwick's edited volume (1937), *Papers on the Science of Administration,* reflects the "organization as machine" metaphor in many different ways. All organizations, public and private, are viewed as machines where conflict signals a breakdown, a deficiency. Like a machine, all the parts of the organization—or government—must work together. Therefore, the key to administrative efficiency is "coordination" and singleness of purpose. Harmony signals that all is well.

The importance of coordination and singleness of purpose is noted by Mooney and Reiley in 1931: "This term expresses the principles of organization in toto; nothing else. This does not mean that there are no subordinated principles; it simply means that all the others are contained in this one of co-ordination. The others are simply the principles through which co-ordination operates, and thus becomes effective" (cited in Urwick, 1937a, p. 49).

The council-manager form extends the depoliticization of administrative processes into the political sphere (Haber, 1964). Unifying powers rather than separating them creates the assumption as well as the image of the community as a harmonious unit with a single purpose. This belief is reflected in the view that the governing body should operate as a unit and in the way the council-manager form structures elections that are nonpartisan and focused on local issues rather than on party labels and national politics. In addition, the governing body came to be elected at large under the assumption that individuals make a difference in government and that individuals with a community-wide perspective are better qualified to serve than those advocating a special interest or constituency. Further, council members would serve part-time, with little or no pay, signifying an end to the professional politician.

In addition, the council-manager form envisions a governing body headed by a mayor selected by its members—preferably business leaders (Stone, Price, and Stone, 1940) who work during the day and are willing to serve the community in repayment for their economic good fortune. The mayor's role is designated as ceremonial rather than political, further signifying the importance of harmony and unity among the governing body.

In sum, one can see how the value of efficiency came to play such an important part in the orthodox view of council-manager government. It supports the idea of the manager as expert; it fosters a link between the structure of the corporation and government; and it implies the view that the public interest is achieved through cooperation, planning, and discovery of the public good.

Conclusions

According to Stillman (1974), council-manager government blended two streams of Progressive thought. On the one hand, by reducing the number of elected officials and focusing political authority in the hands of a small governing body elected at large, representative democracy could be invigorated and machine politics weakened. On the other hand, by focusing administrative authority in the hands of a city manager, centralized planning and rational approaches to public problems could be enhanced. Five decades earlier, White (1927) had written that "the council-manager plan . . . is the most perfect expression which the American people have yet evolved of the need for combining efficient administration with adequate popular control" (p. 295).

In many ways, the strength of council-manager government lies in the blending of an impersonal governmental structure with normative value. Council-manager government worked pragmatically to reduce the impact of machine politics and bring rational problem solving to government. But perhaps more important, it was a pragmatism infused with intellectual and moral appeal. Thus, while many specific features of the council-manager design and the role of the city manager have changed over several decades, the symbols that reflect the intellectual and moral appeal largely remain a part of contemporary public discourse about council-manager government.

Despite its intellectual and moral appeal, from its inception council-manager government was vulnerable to attack from those who charged that administrative power frequently challenged political control, that small governing bodies were not representative of all citizens, and that council-manager government impeded the rise of political leadership. Chapter Two describes these charges.

2

Challenges to the Council-Manager Ideal

Council-manager government was designed in the early 1900s to promote two goals. First, it aimed to improve political responsiveness by eliminating machine politics and focusing political accountability in a small nonpartisan governing body. Second, it sought to increase efficiency in government by centralizing administrative activities in the position of the city manager, a trained administrative expert who would serve at the pleasure of the governing body.

Accompanying these goals was a supportive intellectual orthodoxy that separated politics from administration, portrayed administration as a politically neutral activity, and highlighted efficiency as a dominant administrative value. The design of council-manager government and this orthodox view stimulated criticism in its early years, and a full-fledged attack on scientific management and administrative science in general occurred in the 1940s (Appleby, 1949; Simon, [1945] 1976; Waldo, 1984). Contemporary political forces have eroded the seemingly indestructible orthodoxy as well.

This chapter identifies the complex political environment that faces council-manager government today. Then, focusing on recent illustrations, it gives voice to the critics of council-manager government. Criticism of council-manager government falls into three major areas: first, that it gives too much power to the city manager and administrative staff; second, that it fails to promote political leadership and accountability; and third, that it frustrates political representation for minority citizens and viewpoints.

Contemporary Political Environments

Newland (1989) contrasts today's "transactional" politics with the ideal of "transformational" politics (Burns, 1978). Transactional politics are conflict-oriented and marked by narrow interests; political processes are designed to mediate conflict rather than produce long-range public policy. In contrast, collaborative, community-oriented politics with a "civic culture of integrity and informed achievement" characterize transformational politics.

Newland (1989) observes that changes in the structure of local governments reflect and reinforce conflict-oriented politics. For example, he cites increased district versus at-large elections, independent council staff, and greater compensation for council members as departures from the ideal environment and transformational politics. Sharp (1989) adds: "Perhaps it is useful to say that reform has become more complex, and that the principles of professionalism, nonpartisanship, and centralized, merit-based management must be worked out within a context that places greater emphasis on particularistic interests" (p. 5).

Political Diversity. Increased diversity of community interests bearing on public policy might be cautiously inferred from the following information in two different surveys. In an ICMA survey in 1971 (Barrett & Harmon, 1972, p. 11), respondents in council-manager cities, when asked to indicate the frequency of contact between council members and various other members of the council's role set, placed neighborhood groups in a tie for fourth among six choices. In a National League of Cities survey (1980, p. 15) conducted in 1979, respondents were asked which groups had "considerable or some" influence on public policy. Respondents listed neighborhood groups as the most influential in both council-manager and strong-mayor cities. These survey results support in-depth work by Sharp (1986) and Thomas (1986) that documents the activities of neighborhood groups in Kansas City and Cincinnati. Especially in larger municipalities, officials today are elected from a broad array of backgrounds. Robert Kipp (1987), former city manager in Kansas City, Missouri, and past president of the ICMA, describes the challenge diversity poses this way: "The governing bodies of these large cities are much more diverse and far more representative of the real city than they used to be. But because they are more diverse, they pose new and different problems for a manager. It's much more difficult to find common ground and develop consensus" (p. 113).

Diversity raises concern for representation not only in important areas such as how governing bodies are elected, but even in those areas that may seem inconsequential. For example, in November 1988, Mayor Annette Strauss of Dallas proposed that in order to provide greater focus on the arts, a city department of cultural affairs be separated from its current home in the Parks and Recreation Department. Park Board member Rene Martinez cautioned that the current emphasis on cultural and racial diversity might be threatened in a separate department. Four months later, according to the *Dallas Morning News* (Housewright, 1989), a minority spokesperson in the arts community voiced stronger concern, asserting that "the arts department 'should be under the park board so that African-American, Hispanic and other ethnic arts institutions will receive parity in funding based on census population and growing ethnic diversity.'"

Professional Politicians and Special Interests. It is not only broader diversity that challenges consensus building. According to Ehrenhalt (1988), the nature of the local government elected official has changed as well. Based on his familiarity with local government and his in-depth study of the San Francisco Bay Area city of Concord, Ehrenhalt describes the rapid change from amateur to professional politician. For part-time council members, he writes that "a job in private life is simply a way to make a political career possible. It is a means not an end" (p. 53). He further observes that "they [politicians in Concord] do not win office because they are leaders. They become leaders by virtue of holding office" (p. 53).

Narrow political interests mediated by conflict-oriented processes spearheaded by not-so-amateur elected leaders produce a context alien to the community-wide perspective that the council-manager plan assumes. Yates (1977) has observed that the multiplicity of participants with articulated interests in urban policy "imposes high transaction costs and makes it all the more difficult for city government to make coherent decisions—or for that matter any decisions at all" (p. 118). Jewel Scott (1987), city manager in Delaware, Ohio, adds: "One of the things that I have seen in my community and that I think is happening in cities is a tendency toward segmentation of interests. There have always been the special interest groups . . . but I think we are seeing those groups become much more defined and narrowly focused" (p. 208).

Norman Hickey (1987), administrator of Hillsborough County, Florida, expresses his opinion that "you have to justify basic issues rather than just say, 'The administrator proposed it.' The fact that you are a person of integrity is no longer taken for granted or if it is it just is not worth very much when it comes to getting one's way with an elected body" (pp. 88–89).

Administrative Power and Accountability

Against this backdrop of diversity, professional politicians, and special interests, the debate over the city manager's role concentrates on administrative power and accountability. How insulated from community politics should administrators be? How can a government structure itself to ensure bureaucratic responsiveness to appropriate political leadership?

Administrative Neutrality. Administrative neutrality purposefully isolates bureaucrats from political interference. The result is that bureaucrats accrue power from their monopoly on information, from the day-to-day discretion they exercise, and from their steadfast commitment to bureaucratic standards of performance. From the bureaucrat's perspective and for those who adhere strongly to the concept of administrative neutrality this protection is virtuous. The politician, however, may regard this concept with skepticism.

In Chapter One we saw how the concept of administrative

neutrality held center stage in the orthodox view of city management. It grew out of the proposition that politics and administration were separate spheres of action. In return for protection from partisan political influence, administrative staff were obligated to recommend and carry out public policy in a politically neutral fashion—that is, without a partisan political bias.

Advocates of professionalism and the council-manager form are quick to protect administrators from political influence whether partisan or not. For example, in Kansas City, Missouri, which is a strong council-manager city, an editorialist for the *Kansas City Times* ("Council vs. Bureaucrats," 1988) responds to council charges that "professional government is running wild" thus: "Actually, it seems more likely that these council members are crying about their own inability to get things done exactly the way they want at City Hall. They are inconvenienced by city employees who, armed with facts and intelligence, too often tell them their ideas aren't workable." In fact, nine months later, the *Kansas City Times* ("A Better City Budget Next Time," 1989) counseled: "Olson [David Olson, city manager] and his staff are supposed to be the experts who understand the numbers and how they translate to services for residents. They shouldn't hesitate to suggest cuts in programs no matter how politically unpopular they will be. Don't count votes all the time. Being bold and stating how government really should function is not so bad. Olson's more timid approach has not exactly helped him with his critics on the council."

The endorsement of an orthodox view of administrative independence from politics is seen also in Dallas, where columnist Philip Seib (1989) writes: "If Dallas' council-manager system . . . is to work properly, council members should establish basic policy guidelines, approve the budget and not meddle in the daily workings of the city. The separation of powers must be maintained." He continues: "Despite the problems that inevitably plague any city of almost a million residents, Dallas runs relatively well, especially when the council members and the city manager respect each other's prerogatives. Recent City Hall inefficiency is likely due, at least in part, to council members' interference in the manager's business."

Politicians may develop a less sanguine view of administrative neutrality. The politician in the council-manager form serves part-time, and the bureaucrat's access to information and exercise of discretion may frustrate the council member's oversight function. The bureaucrat's protection from political influence and general separation from politics make the politician's promise of providing constituent services dependent upon bureaucratic goodwill. Finally, the politician's role representing the policy interests of constituents may be thwarted by bureaucrats "armed with facts and intelligence." In short, if one accepts these differences in perspective between the bureaucrat and politician, one could argue that *as they see it,* politicians control few resources as they approach their relationship with staff (Krislov and Rosenbloom, 1981; Price, 1965).

Power of the City Manager. Svara (1985, 1990) has described the relationship between the city manager and the governing body as a partnership, with the council as senior partner. From the critic's perspective, one sees a lay governing body vulnerable to the power of the city manager and administrative staff.

Both journalistic accounts and recent research show that city managers have access to significant resources available to the governing body only through the manager. Coile (1988) prepared a journalistic account of city government in Tucson, concentrating on the role of a long-time, powerful city manager, Joel Valdez. She observes: "Tucson is a council-manager system, meaning the seven-member city council sets public policy and can remove Valdez. But it is up to Valdez to put the council's policies into action and control day-to-day operations, and in practice, he is the most powerful person in city government" (p. 47).

Recent research supports Coile's journalistic observations. Abney and Lauth (1982), in their 1978 survey of fire chiefs, police chiefs, and public works directors in cities with populations over 50,000, found that "department heads in the council-manager form of government . . . regard the chief executive as having more impact upon them than the city council" (pp. 136–137). With regard to the budget, Abney and Lauth (1986, p. 143) found that city managers "clearly" had more influence over council members than did mayors.

City managers tend to downplay their role as policymakers. In large measure, they justify the negotiating and brokering they do in the community, with the council, and within their own staff as nonpolitical problem solving subject, in the final analysis, to council approval. From the elected official's perspective, however, the test of accountability comes from the informal process of governing as well as the formal. According to an ICMA survey of city managers, 87 percent of the respondents indicated that they "always" set their council's agenda (Green, 1987, p. 3). Abney and Lauth (1982) found that 90 percent of the chief executives, including city managers, in cities of over 50,000 population had the power to propose the budget. More important, they found empirically that "the power to propose a budget is an essential power needed to gain influence" (p. 137). Control of the budget translates into control over information, which often is the source of tension between council members and professional staff. Even when shared with council, the derivation of the information and the context within which it is developed are frequently unknown to council members. Coile's account (1988) of Valdez in Tucson illustrates this problem: "Valdez is best known for his ironclad control over the city's budget. Wheeler [a council member] says he was warned by another councilman that Valdez lets the council affect about 2 percent of the budget, which totals $498 million for fiscal 1988–1989. 'Absolutely, he controls the budget,' says Council Member Miller. 'You gotta have a little sense of humor about that. . . . You come to a budget meeting and okay, today you're going to discuss the library. Here it is $12 million. You have x number of libraries, you have so much for this and that. Unless you've worked in the library department— like Joel has, by the way—you don't know what's going on there. . . . When it's all said and done with these departments, how do I know how many people Valdez needs for maintenance?' " (p. 49).

The answer, of course, is that council members do not know, and the city manager would probably add that they do not need to know. But whether the council needs to know or not, the governing body's largely unspoken concern is with its *feeling of dependence* on the manager and professional staff. If not handled carefully by staff, this feeling leads to charges of professional arrogance.

David Watkins (1986), city administrator in suburban Lenexa, Kansas, acknowledges the manager's responsibility in this regard: "Council must rely on staff recommendations in order to create effective policies. This authority to recommend policy gives a city manager power, and in some cities it is absolute power. It is very easy to abuse your authority. A good manager will have complete trust from the governing body so without some type of personal or professional value base, abuses can happen."

Jewel Scott (1987) shows the same sensitivity: "[Managers] can lose touch with the community because they get so wrapped up in their professional opinion, the facts, and their personal opinions that they really don't provide the kind of community management they should. It becomes more management for managers as opposed to management for the people. I think it's a little easier for that to happen to us than it is to an elected council because the council's stated role is to represent those people in a community" (p. 213).

Distrust of Professional Staff. While Watkins and Scott acknowledge their power and the dangers of abuse, from the critic's perspective the city manager's power may only reveal the tip of a bureaucratic iceberg. Department heads formally do not set the council's agenda nor do they propose the budget, but they probably have more tenure in office than the city manager or the council members. Power accrues to those who know what has and has not worked in the past and why; and with history comes experience and acquisition of specialized knowledge: of management information systems, of utility operations, of solid waste disposal, of federal housing programs, of accounting procedures and investment practices, of water distribution, of land use planning, of legal liability and risk management, and the list goes on.

The suspicion that critical council members harbor toward government bureaucracy centers in large measure on the monopoly that bureaucrats have over information and the discretion they exercise. Their unease can be seen in newspaper reports like one from Gresham, Oregon, a council-manager city, where the *Oregonian* (Carman, 1988) quotes Don McIntire, an advocate of a strong mayor system: "McIntire said some community members fear the part-time mayor and unpaid council members rely too heavily on city employees because city business has grown complex. When we have people who are setting policy, even though setting policy isn't in their job description, then that person ought to be accountable to the electorate. . . . Pretty soon, the council becomes yes-men for the employees instead of the other way around."

Another example of the distrust stemming from staff control over information comes from Dallas. After newspaper reports detailed the controversial renovation of a low-cost housing complex, council member Jerry Rucker minced no words when, despite their denial, he scolded staff by saying they had hidden information from the council. According to the *Dallas Morning News* (Flournoy, May 18, 1989), Rucker said: "The system of public government by elected representatives has been purposefully subverted. . . . And now with all the stink all over them they are coming in and saying, 'Gosh, I'm sorry fellas.' . . . But it isn't that accidental folks. It was done on purpose."

In addition to the near monopoly staff has over information, it also exercises discretion that critics say may challenge council oversight and supremacy. Gruber (1987) observes in her study of fire departments, housing departments, and education departments in non–council-manager cities: "The world of bureaucrats is filled with administrative matters, technical services, substantive programs and job satisfactions or dissatisfaction—not with political issues or the search to implement democratic norms" (p. 102). She concludes that while bureaucrats can voice appropriate democratic values, they do not live them. They simply do not see themselves as involved in democratic processes.

Desire for Independent Information. The critical council expresses its distrust of professional staff in at least two ways: the desire for independent sources of information and the desire to get involved in administration. For example, in association with a housing controversy in Dallas, council member Charles Tandy (Flournoy, May 2, 1989) is reported to have said, "Evidence continues to pile up that the city staff has been less than totally honest with us." The report continued: "He [Tandy] will ask City Auditor Dan Paul to conduct a full investigation of the Twelve Hills deal. The council member said asking Mr. Knight's [city manager] office to examine the rental rehabilitation program is the same as having the 'wolf investigating the henhouse.' " On a charter review issue in Dallas, the *Dallas Morning News* (Crawford and Housewright, 1989) reports council

skeptic Diane Ragsdale as saying she supported a delay in the charter panel's work because she "wants to get information from an
'independent demographer that we can trust.' " Kansas City council
member Shields (Fitzpatrick, 1989), reported to be an administration critic, voiced a similar concern when she "eschewed the assistance of City Budget Officer Verlyn Leiker and called on City
Auditor Mark Funkhouser to calculate the cost of some budgetary
alternatives. Funkhouser works for the council, while Leiker is the
administration's fiscal guru."

Council Involvement in Administration. In addition to the desire
for independent information, critical council members increasingly
seem to want to be involved in administration. For example, the
Kansas City Times (Fitzpatrick, 1988) reported: "Aiming for control
over who gets lucrative city bond work, three Kansas City Council
members have proposed that the council, not the city staff, select
law firms and investment banking firms to help the city issue bonds
for a possible expansion of Bartle Hall." This contrasts with past
practice where city staff would make the selection, which "avoided
even the appearance that political favors were being traded." Svara's
research has led him to conclude: "At the same time that managers
provide more policy leadership, they are experiencing more incursion from council members interested in being ombudsmen with
regard to services and in using management practices to advance
policy ends (e.g., minority contracting requirements). In these respects, the manager as expert is also being challenged in 'his' or
'her' own sphere" (letter to the author, Dec. 1987).

Political Leadership and Accountability

The second major tension in council-manager government is the
charge that it fails to encourage political leadership and accountability. However, the vacuum in political leadership, which city
managers themselves criticize, is not unique to the council-manager
plan. It seems that whenever citizens in the United States feel that
they are losing control, whether in their personal lives or their
politics, the response is the same—seek leadership! The renewed
emphasis on leadership in private business is just as strong as it is

in the public sector. Leadership seems to be a political and administrative remedy, but it is not always clear what problem it is supposed to address.

Thus, a precise discussion of the lack of political leadership in the council-manager form of government is difficult to assemble. Nevertheless, a review of the history of the council-manager plan reveals continual concern for the lack of quality and political focus on the governing body (Strauss Pealy, 1958; White, 1927). One of the goals of reformers at the turn of the century was to remove the negative aspects of politics—the corruption, political machines, patronage—from local government. They invented a structure of government that would help accomplish this: they promoted nonpartisan and eventually at-large elections, part-time politicians, and a mayor selected from within the governing body to fulfill largely ceremonial functions.

In large measure they succeeded, but not without cost. In the same vein that one cannot depoliticize a city and still represent the views of all citizens to their own satisfaction (Adrian, 1988), one cannot expect strong political leadership consistently within the governing body when the structure is designed to minimize the negative effects of politics (Strauss Pealy, 1958). Managers complain that the lack of political leadership can be attributed to the people who run for office today. But the structure of council-manager government may not facilitate or encourage strong political leadership.

Even though there are disagreements about whether a strong mayor-council form of government is a prerequisite to strong political leadership (Svara, 1990), the need for political focus in local government is acknowledged by city manager, critic, and academic alike. Robert Kipp (1987; see Bonsey, 1987, and Foell, 1987, for other examples) says: "'Should we have a strong mayor government or a city manager government?' That issue is artificial because you need strong political leadership wherever you can possibly attain it. You need both a strong mayor and professional management" (p. 113).

The call for focused political leadership seems particularly evident in cities where major redevelopment, adversarial politics, or deep-seated social conflict is present (Banfield and Wilson, 1966; Sparrow, 1985). Journalist Anthony Lukas (1988) describes what he sees as the need for a strong mayor in Yonkers, a highly politicized council-manager city and the home of a particularly divisive and bitter battle with the courts over the initiation of low-cost housing: "Yonkers has a weak mayor system of government. With no administrative power and little patronage, the mayor is largely a ceremonial figure—essentially a councilman who must run citywide. Administrative power rests with the city manager, who has some patronage but little political influence. Nobody has sufficient clout to grapple with the twin specters of race and class" (p. 2).

Blending into the critique of political leadership on councils is concern for accountability. Critics who call for a strong mayor, for example, argue that when citizens are dissatisfied, they should have one political target. Now, they claim, responsibility gets buried within the governing body and passed back and forth between the council and the city manager. Further, critics, analysts, and managers themselves acknowledge that without strong political leadership, the manager may step into the void and become the true policy leader (Gaebler, 1987; Protasel, 1988; Sanders, 1982).

Newspaper reports from Fort Collins, Colorado, and Toledo, Ohio, provide illustrations of contemporary demands for more political leadership and political accountability in the council-manager form of government. The *Fort Collins Coloradoan* ("End Charade; Elect Mayor," 1989), in the third of a series of editorials about the city's future, suggests: "Today's theme is the lack of and need for community leadership. . . . No one in Fort Collins is in a position to lead. The mayor is the mayor of the City Council, not of the city. . . . The current form of government provides no constituency base [for the mayor], no continuity, no focus, no leadership. . . . Focus the leadership. Put someone clearly in charge. That someone should be elected by the people, not hired by a council. . . . A big city needs a strong, directly elected mayor working full-time (at full-time pay) with a four-year term."

Adding to this view are the comments from Fort Collins council member Susan Kirkpatrick ("Directly Elected Mayor . . . ," 1989): "We allow that person [the mayor who is selected by the council] to appear on behalf of the council. . . . But we don't allow that person truly to speak for us unless we've taken a vote on something or there's clear consensus." She continues: "Other cities use a city manager with a directly elected mayor who has the opportunity to campaign citywide . . . [and] also offer the winner the opportunity to speak about and for the community as a whole. Our current system doesn't allow anybody to do that."

While Fort Collins has recently begun to think seriously about modifying its council-manager form, in Toledo the campaign to abandon council-manager government has been tested many times. The essence of the message in Toledo, led by the *Toledo Blade,* is twofold. First, a strong mayor would provide a focal point for political leadership; second, a strong mayor could be held accountable for failures of governance. This message is summarized aptly in the *Blade* ("For Strong Mayor System," 1989) which, preceding an election to change the charter, editorialized:

> A city is an organic entity, like a state or a country. It has to have a sense of mission, a set of goals and far-seeing leaders. Its residents must have some sense of the public good and a sense of community.
>
> The council-manager form of government . . . offers none of these. Council often shrinks from exercising real leadership because it is reluctant to tread upon the manager's administrative prerogatives. The city manager frequently is reluctant to recommend policy because he or she fears to tread upon the Council's legislative prerogatives.
>
> Responsiveness and courageous leadership is what is sorely lacking in the present system of Toledo municipal government. The Council ducks behind the city manager, the city manager hides behind the Council, and the mayor, whose limited powers essentially make him or her the first among equals on the Council, can find it very convenient to duck behind both. The buck stops nowhere.

Despite the abandonment campaign, on November 8, 1989, Toledo voters rejected by nearly nine percentage points a proposition that would have created a strong mayor.

Representation

The discussion of administrative neutrality and political leadership highlights the importance that political control of governmental bureaucracies has for democratic theory. As a rough analogy one might think of the commitment in the United States to civilian control of the military. The concept is the same, whether civil or military: government bureaucracies must answer to the citizens through their elected representatives. No less important is the third challenge to council-manager government—who those representatives are (Friedrich, 1963; Gottdiener, 1987; Lipset in Connolly, 1984). Critics of council-manager government complain that the at-large election of part-time council members discriminates against minority citizens.

As the council-manager plan began to spread during the early part of this century, critics saw it as an attempt by business interests to create a form of government that would conform to a corporate view of the public interest (Banfield and Wilson, 1966; Haber, 1964; Hays, 1964; Hofstadter, 1955). While this view was valued by some, the concept of government as a business was criticized as excluding from political processes the lower class or the "have-nots." At-large elections promised the citywide perspective the reformers sought, but it hindered election of minority representatives. Further, the goal of eliminating professional politicians from municipal politics by making the elected official's role part-time with nominal pay, frustrated working-class candidates whose hours were dictated by an employer and not by civic duty.

The remarkable fact is that these criticisms go to the heart of contemporary criticisms of council-manager government as well. In a small council-manager community like Lawrence, Kansas, one finds a critical letter to the editor (Minkin, 1989) that could have been written some seventy-five years ago:

> Editor: Once again the *Journal-World* is on the front line in defending the position of the rich and powerful. By encouraging foot-dragging and minimal change on the salary increase for city commissioners, you have typically come out four-square in favor of

elitism and protecting us from "the vulgar breath of democracy." Maybe the best possible solution . . . is to add some new requirements to running for city commissioner:

1. Candidates must be business owners, corporate executives, or retired.
2. Absolutely no hourly or salaried employee need apply. Even those able to manipulate their schedules, sacrifice the income, and avoid pressure that may come from management should be excluded.
3. Working or single parents who must find and pay for child care should be prohibited from serving.
4. Those citizens who have chosen a lifestyle and/or vocation that does not reflect a corporate, consumer mindset may not seek office.

The political stakes are a lot higher in Dallas, where a Charter Review Panel considered ways to increase minority representation on the council partly to head off litigation that would force restructuring of the eleven-person council—eight district and three at-large seats, including the mayor's. The city's population is estimated at 1.1 million with roughly half composed of minorities. Even with this large minority population, African Americans or Hispanics fill only three of the eleven seats on the council. The debate over representational issues in charter revision discussions are drawn very clearly along racial lines. The *Dallas Morning News* (Kelley, Feb. 20, 1989) reported that some 55 percent of the respondents in a poll favored creation of more single member districts, with greatest support coming from African Americans and Hispanics who favored the measure by more than 2-to-1 compared to support by only about half of the Anglos surveyed.

During the 1989 mayoral campaign in Dallas, candidate Peter Lesser ran on a platform that supported the views of minority council members Diane Ragsdale and Al Lipscomb. When he announced his candidacy, Lesser said: "We have government of the rich, we have government of the *patrons,* we have a paternalistic system. It's wrong, it's undemocratic." He went on to say that "council members must be full-time representatives, paid a full-time salary, and have a staff they can hire and fire" (Kelley, Feb. 2, 1989).

Ragsdale and Lipscomb, who oppose the council-manager plan and favor district elections, voiced their staunch opposition to the present system. Ragsdale is reported to have said about the current system of at-large elections: "That heightens the political inequity. . . . The issue is how to eliminate oppression, inequity, and injustice" (Housewright, Feb. 26, 1989). On another occasion, she reportedly said of the council-manager system: "It's an elitist and exclusionary system. . . . It exludes minorities and working people. You either have to rely heavily on your family or simply take away from your business a lot" (Housewright and Weiss, Jan. 14, 1989). Lipscomb added that "we have to protest, demonstrate or litigate in this city to make some type of upward movement" (Housewright, Feb. 26, 1989). Columnist Carolyn Barta (Jan. 30, 1989) thoughtfully comments about Ragsdale and Lipscomb: "Council members Ragsdale and Lipscomb are not personality blips on this city radar screen. They represent a constituency—the underclass—that will continue to be represented on the council."

Dallas is not the only place where the council-manager plan is seen as representing the views of established business interests. In an illuminating article about the transition in the character of elected officials in Concord, California, a suburban San Francisco Bay Area municipality, Ehrenhalt (1988) describes the before and after:

> On the outskirts of Concord, overlooking the hills east of town, is an affluent residential street, St. Francis Drive, that is home to four men who served as mayor of the city between 1960 and 1975. It is a symbol of the old political system under which people not only made decisions together, but built houses next door to each other [p. 56].
>
> "When I first came on the City council," says Larry Azevedo, a Republican elected in 1968, "it was like a good-old-boys club. The city manager would call me up and I'd go down to a coffee shop and two

or three other councilmen would be there and we'd
shoot the breeze and do some business."

There was an intimate connection between that
"boys club" and the Chamber of Commerce, which
presided over the community's growth. The Chamber
was the political training ground; most of the time, an
aspiring office holder tried out his leadership skills
there before moving on to elective office [pp. 51–52].

And in suburban Kansas City, David Watkins (1989), city administrator, notes: "In many communities, particularly fast growing
ones, at-large elections are stifling participation of potential leaders, especially new residents, who lack the name identification. In
Olathe [Kansas] . . . three out of five commissioners lived within
one block of each other in a community of over 55,000 people. This
political disenfranchisement of a large part of the community led
to a change in the form of government in an effort to guarantee
ward representation" (p. 274).

Conclusions

The orthodox view of city management influenced and reflected the
design of council-manager government. But in designing government to promote democracy and efficiency, the reformers did not
escape criticism. Contemporary critics as well as their predecessors
charge that council-manager government creates powerful bureaucracies at the expense of political supremacy, obstructs political
focus in the community, and represents mainstream interests better
than minority interests. These criticisms have been consistent over
time, suggesting that they emanate in general from the environment
of municipal government and in part from the design of council-
manager government, and not from the people who are elected and
appointed to serve.

Over several decades, communities throughout the country
have been modifying the council-manager plan to make it conform
with their own rather than history's purposes and politics. The next
chapter describes some of the design changes that have taken place
in council-manager government.

3

Adaptive Responses in Local Government Design

Formal changes in the council-manager plan voted by citizens or a governing body constitute structural adaptations to contemporary political challenges. Social structure is much more flexible than steel girders, but both fill the same purpose—they constitute formal solutions to design problems. In effect, modifications in the design of council-manager government respond to the kinds of challenges discussed in Chapter Two. Each moves the plan away from its original design but brings it into conformity with the political culture in a community.

Adaptations have taken place in the structure of council-manager government and in the roles, responsibilities, and values of city management professionals. These structural and behavioral changes complement each other, and together they have transformed the city management profession. This chapter highlights the office of the mayor, the way the governing body is elected, and structural mechanisms designed to increase responsiveness of the professional staff to the governing body.

Political Leadership

The original ideal of council-manager government had the mayor selected by the governing body from among its members and placed in a purely ceremonial role. A major, though gradual change has occurred with the direct election of the mayor. By adopting the direct election of mayors, many council-manager cities have sought to enhance their capability to focus political leadership. In some cities, the mayor is given power to veto council actions.

Direct election of the mayor is not a recent phenomenon. Childs (1965, pp. 39–40) reported that in 1945, 40 percent of council-manager cities elected their mayor directly. In 1965 the number of cities directly electing the mayor (52 percent) surpassed selection from among the council (48 percent) (Childs, 1965, p. 40). Adrian (1988, p. 10) reports that in 1986, 62 percent of council-manager cities directly elected their mayor.

Limited research on the impact of the direct election of mayor on council-manager government produces mixed and largely dated results. Kammerer (1964) has shown that Florida mayors elected at large tend to limit the discretion of Florida city managers. Booth's research (1968) in small council-manager cities randomly drawn nationwide showed that directly elected mayors had no adverse effects on the operations of council-manager government. Svara's more recent research (1989b), limited to municipalities in North Carolina and Ohio, also shows limited differences. He concludes from survey responses of city managers that "elected mayors are more effective at resolving community conflict. They also command more attention and alter the behavior of the manager and staff more than council-selected mayors. The elected mayor is twice as likely to correct staff performance independently of the council, and four times more likely to be perceived as effective at guiding the administrative activities of the city" (p. 17). But overall, according to Svara, effective mayors are no more likely to have been elected by the citizens than selected from among the council.

Perhaps more important than any possible differences in effectiveness between elected versus chosen mayors is the political symbolism that the direct election of a mayor signifies. Virtually all observers of council-manager government agree that the orthodox view envisioned a ceremonial role for the mayor, presiding over council meetings and serving as titular head of the government. Boynton and Wright (1971) captured the difference between orthodoxy and reality of both the mayor and manager with an attractive analogy: "The images of the offices of the American mayor and the city manager found in the literature of public administration and political science are related to the realities of those offices in much the same way as Smokey the Bear is related to the grizzly bear of the Northwest" (p. 28).

In fact, the mayor's role has broadened significantly, with its centrality reflected symbolically if not actually in citizens' desire to directly elect the mayor. Most generally, research shows that the mayor's role in council-manager government focuses on providing political leadership. Wikstrom (1979) reports, "The position of mayor in Virginia cities is viewed by most of those who seek office, or wish to retain it, as a central vantage point through which they can influence the policy process" (p. 273). Svara (1989b) notes that the effective mayor acts to coordinate communication and to organize and provide policy guidance. Boynton and Wright (1971) found: "Mayors stand out as political actors who differ dramatically from other members of the council. They are more likely to (1) have the most contact with political party leaders; (2) be nominated as the major political leader in the city; (3) be consulted by the manager about political issues; and (4) most frequently be involved in the administrative process in the city—with involvement measured as oversight of and contact with administrative officials" (p. 30).

Boynton and Wright (1971), Svara (1989b), and Wikstrom (1979) have shown that mayoral success in council-manager cities grows out of a cooperative relationship with other governmental actors—the manager/professional staff and others on the council. There is virtually no argument among scholars that the partnership that marks effective mayor-manager relations expands both the mayor's and the manager's role beyond that envisioned in the orthodox view of city management, in which politics and administration were seen as distinct spheres of activity.

While the directly elected mayor symbolizes the expanded role of the mayor, failure to spotlight the role may have significant detrimental effects on support for council-manager government. Booth (1968) speculated in his study of the mayor's office in small council-manager cities, that, as in national and state politics, the popular election of chief local executives may be an important part of the American political ethic. He observes that failure to include the direct election of the mayor in municipal charters may risk their defeat.

Along this same line, Protasel (1988) concludes that the presence of a directly elected mayor appears to affect positively the viability of the council-manager plan. He surveyed all cities that had abandoned the council-manager form of government during 1976–1986 and found that only 26 percent of the abandonments had occurred in cities in which the voters directly elected the mayor.

Protasel's study (1989) of mayoral veto power leads him to caution that mayors elected at large are beginning to serve as a check and balance against council actions. For example, he points out that while only 2 percent of mayors selected from among the council have a veto power, 21 percent of those elected at large have some veto authority. In addition, he notes that 40 percent of the directly elected mayors can vote only in case of a council tie. In contrast, only 3 percent of the mayors selected from among the council are limited to voting only in case of a council tie.

In sum, there appear to be few obstacles to the gradual trend in the direct election of mayors in the council-manager government. Furthermore, while mayoral effectiveness is not conclusively enhanced by direct election, the directly elected mayor symbolizes the focus on political leadership that council-manager government has often been challenged as lacking.

Representation

As the percentage of the minority population in communities increases, the political pressure for increased representation increases as well. There are numerous ways of promoting representation, including the use of representative citizen task forces, boards, and commissions, as well as the sensitivity that professional managers and staff show toward citizen participation (Streib, 1990). But representation on the governing body signifies most visibly minority political power.

Criticisms of council-manager government and at-large elections were primarily political in the 1960s, in the aftermath of urban unrest and riots, and then legal, as when in 1986 the Supreme Court ruled in *Thornburg* v. *Gingles* against at-large elections that produced discriminatory patterns of representation. In 1968 the *Report of the National Advisory Commission on Civil Disorders* (Kerner Commission) concluded after looking into the urban unrest, that "city manager government has eliminated an important political link between city government and low-income residents" (cited in Mulrooney, 1971, p. 8). The social unrest and statements like that of the Kerner Commission renewed thinking about the relationship between council-manager government, representation, and social equity (Banovetz, 1971; Mulrooney, 1971; *Managing for Social and Economic Opportunity*, 1969).

In *Thornburg* v. *Gingles* (1986), the Supreme Court was asked to apply the Voting Rights Act of 1965 as amended to redistricting that had taken place in North Carolina in 1982. The Court ruled that an electoral method that produces discriminatory results violates the Act. Lack of intent to discriminate does not protect a jurisdiction's electoral process if it impairs the ability of minorities to elect representatives of their choice.

In March 1990 the United States District Court in Dallas ruled that the separate elections of eight members of the governing body by district, three at large, and the mayor at large diluted the political strength of minorities. Judge Buchmeyer ordered the city to present a new plan more representative of Dallas's minority population. In late April the city council voted to present a 12-1 plan to the Court. In addition to specific litigation, the newest edition of the National Civic League's (1989) Model City Charter adopted in 1989 recognizes for the first time district elections as an alternative to the at-large method.

As a consequence of political pressure and litigation, cities have moved away from strictly at-large or district systems for mixed systems. Renner's analysis (1987) in Table 1, which compares methods of election in council-manager cities in 1971, 1981, and 1986, shows that regardless of the form of government, a decline has occurred in at-large elections for all groups of cities with a population over 2,500. This decline has occurred in all geographic regions. In addition, again discounting the form of government, his analysis shows that there are relatively few municipalities, regardless of population size, that have purely district elections. Smaller population

cities prefer at-large systems, with larger population cities prefer-
ring a mixed or ward system.

Renner (1987) also observes that the method of election has
little impact on African American representation in cities with less
than 20 percent African American population. In contrast, the
larger the African American population, the more impact the method of election has on the number of African Americans elected to
council seats.

Although not broken down by form of government, Schellinger's analysis (1988) of ICMA data shows that the number of minority council members has increased modestly but fairly steadily since
1971 (see Table 2). The percentage of minority council members
appears to be directly related to city size and presumably to percentage of minority population. For example, in 1986 in cities with a
population of 500,000 and over, 22.4 percent of the council members
were African American and 6.0 Hispanic. In contrast, in cities under
2,500, only .8 percent were African American and .7 Hispanic.

In sum, political pressure, sensitivity to social issues, and
litigation have brought at-large elections in particular under scrutiny and attack and have steadily increased the number of minority
members of governing bodies.

Table 1. Method of Electing Representatives, 1971–1986.

	Method of Election		
Year	At-Large	Ward	Mixed
1971	76%	24%	1%
1981	76%	8%	16%
1986	68%	6%	26%

Table 2. Percent Minority Council Members, 1971–1986.

	African American	Hispanic
1971	3.2	NA
1974	2.8	NA
1981	3.5	1.3
1986	4.1	1.7

Professionalism

The critique of professionalism centers on the dependence of elected officials upon staff. In council-manager government professional staff can monopolize knowledge, although they are expected to marshal their expertise to assist the governing body.

Managers and staff employ numerous vehicles to provide elected officials access to expertise and policy guidance. Study sessions, goal-setting retreats, an informative agenda packet, council guidance on administrative appointments, electronic mail, and a norm of responsiveness serve these purposes. More fundamental structural changes are designed to advance these purposes as well, but there are few data readily available to catalogue the changes. Survey data (Newell, Glass, and Ammons, 1989, p. 103) do show that, as of 1988, in cities of 50,000 or greater population ($N = 140$), more than 90 percent provide some staff support for the mayor and council. Larger cities more frequently provide independent staff members for the council. In some larger council-manager cities, one finds a professional auditor and staff working for the governing body, providing it with financial information and conducting performance audits at the governing body's request. In addition, initiatives like action centers and neighborhood liaison officers have sought to increase bureaucratic responsiveness.

However, even with behavioral and structural modifications designed to reduce the dependency of elected officials on professional staff, it would be a mistake to infer declining interest in the efficient and equitable delivery of services. Even while voters endorse more political focus through elected mayors, narrower political interests reflected in district elections, and more scrutiny of professional staff, they do not reject professionalism in public policy-making and service delivery. The desire to bring rational analysis to public policy-making and evaluation and to maintain impartial, dependable service delivery leads voters to endorse council-manager government time and again.

Sanders (1982) has shown that from 1970 to 1981 the council-manager plan was abandoned in only 3.5 percent of the cities using it. This figure compares to a 10 percent abandonment in mayor-council cities during the same period. Based on information submitted to it, the International City Management Association (Olander, 1985) reports that from 1980 to 1985 seventy-five municipalities held council-manager referendums, and in sixteen (or some 20 percent) of these cases the plan was abandoned. With 2,543 council-manager cities counted in 1985, this number of abandonments is minuscule.

Charter Reform in Dallas

Recent charter reform in Dallas provides an opportunity to see how one of the largest council-manager cities responded structurally to contemporary political challenges by incorporating or reinforcing some of the changes described so far. Structural changes in government occur in a dynamic political environment where advocates test their political strength. In a politically charged campaign one proposal often invites counter proposals, and reform frequently reflects the interplay between conflicting forces advocating strong political leadership, minority representation, and professionalism (Kaufman, 1956).

The charter review committee that convened in the spring of 1989 sought opinions about city government from over ninety organizations that represented diverse interests in Dallas. The primary purpose of the review was to develop a proposal that would enable city government to represent minority populations effectively. But in the course of its deliberations the committee responded to a variety of criticisms. In the summer of 1989 residents of Dallas adopted the revisions proposed by the committee, although litigation has placed the election results in limbo.

The committee was faced with several fundamental questions of governance: How should citizens choose their representatives and whose views should they represent? How powerful should the mayor be? How insulated should rank-and-file bureaucrats be from political influence?

Proposals to Increase Political Leadership. The committee anticipated that an increase in political fragmentation might occur because of its proposal to increase the size of the governing body and thereby add more district seats. Dallas already elects its mayor at large, and the committee endorsed the unification of legislative and executive power when it rejected a short-lived proposal to give the mayor veto power. To increase the mayor's power, the committee proposed an extension in the mayor's term from two to four years (limited to two terms), thus distinguishing it from the two-year term of council members. In addition, the mayor would be charged with presenting a "state of the city" address annually. Also, the mayor's salary would be set at $2,500 a month in contrast to the $1,650 for council members.

Importantly, in an attempt to reduce the narrow focus and political fragmentation produced by numerous district elections, the committee proposed that agenda items other than those routinely prepared by the city manager be worked through council committees prior to open discussion by the council. Processing by committee is an attempt to discuss and reconcile differences in a small-group work setting rather than before television cameras where political posturing is common. The mayor is granted powers akin to those of the presiding officer of a formal legislative body. These powers include appointment, removal, and naming of chairs of all council committees as well as the power to appoint chairs of boards and commissions.

Proposals to Increase Minority Representation. Prior to the reform, Dallas elected eight representatives by district, two at large, and the mayor at large. A vocal minority proposed twelve single member districts with the mayor elected at large. The majority, seeking to maintain some of the at-large character on the governing body, sought a compromise by increasing the number of representatives on the governing body to fifteen, including ten local districts, four regional districts, and the mayor at large. The four regional districts would have divided the city into four quadrants, expressing broader community interests than those of the other district representatives.

Against the backdrop of a pending lawsuit challenging the existing method of electing the governing body, the bulk of the committee's work and discussion in the newspaper centered around how the proposals would affect minority representation. Ultimately, the committee's majority proposal was presented to the voters, who approved the reform package. However, in March 1990, the

United States District Court ruled against the existing 8-3-1 plan, ordering the city to develop a new plan for electing a more representative governing body and putting the election results on hold.

The committee also approved other features designed to enhance representation. It increased the size of the Park Board and most other boards and commissions, giving additional appointment power to individual council members, guided by a policy that boards and commissions be representative of the racial and ethnic makeup of the city. In addition, in order to meet the criticism that the poor and working class could not afford to spend as much time as required for council duty, the charter committee proposed increasing pay for council members from $50 per meeting to $1,650 per month.

Maintaining Professionalism. The committee endorsed professionalism more by the proposals it rejected than those it included. It could have politicized the bureaucracy in a number of ways, enhancing either the executive authority of the mayor or the power of the council. But it recognized a need for objective analysis and professional management of a multi-million-dollar municipal enterprise.

By maintaining the city manager's accountability to the council rather than to the mayor, the proposal reinforces the charter review committee's belief that executive as well as legislative authority should flow from the city council alone. This ensures that the council has access to professional expertise. Without this access, the council would suffer substantial decline in power no matter how representative it might become or how its representatives are elected.

In contrast, the committee signaled caution to professional staff by establishing a council oversight committee to provide the governing body with an independent assessment of bureaucratic performance. In addition, a provision allowing council members to hire their own staff to serve at the council member's pleasure attempts to increase independence of the council from the professional bureaucracy.

In sum, the charter amendments attempt to strengthen political leadership within the framework of council-manager government; they attempt to represent vigorously minority viewpoints by providing a representative governing body; they attempt to enhance the governing body's ability to generate its own information about public policy proposals and bureaucratic performance; and they endorse the desire to deliver services equitably and conduct governmental business honestly and professionally. Obviously, the proposal does not optimize all these objectives. Charter reform requires compromises of political objectives.

The story of charter reform in Dallas did not end with the election in 1989. Clearly, in Dallas representational and equity issues are paramount, especially in the minority community. Despite the charter election and passage of the 10-4-1 method of constituting the governing body to go into effect in 1991, litigation on the 8-3-1 method was pending. In March 1990 United States District Court Judge Buchmeyer ruled against the 8-3-1 method, and the council picked up on his cue that the 10-4-1 method might not pass judicial scrutiny. With a narrow 6-5 margin the council decided in April to send a 12-1 method, a compromise between 10-1 and 14-1, to the Judge. Minority representatives asserted that the 10-1 or 12-1 method would not ensure adequate representation for African Americans and Hispanics, and they dissented. In fact, the issue has become so polarized that an angry spokesperson for the litigants said: "We expected this. . . . We still have a racist system seated in Dallas, and they expressed that. We've always relied on the consciousness of a federal court to make any gains in Dallas. We've never gotten anything out of this chamber here of any benefit to people of color" (Ragland, Apr. 26, 1990). Then, in September 1990, as part of an agreement with the litigants, the council decided to propose a 14-1 plan to the public in a December referendum. That plan met opposition from advocates who asserted that the city should stick with the 10-4-1 plan that the people adopted by election in 1989. In December the 14-1 referendum was defeated, but in January 1991 the federal district judge ordered the city to hold an election in May based on the 14-1 plan.

A broad view of the political landscape in contemporary local government provides a context for understanding the structural reforms in Dallas or those that appear in other council-manager governments. There is little surprise found in the desire for political focus and leadership, and governing bodies that represent racial minority and narrow political interests. Also unsurprising is governing bodies' skepticism of professional expertise coupled with a seemingly contradictory desire for efficient and equitable service delivery. Structures of local government are recognizing and accommodating these forces.

The Missing Ingredient

Adrian (1988) and Anderson (1989) suggest the adaptive quality of structural change, showing how the features of council-manager and strong-mayor cities appear to be converging. Anderson goes further, implying the positive effect these changes have on legitimizing council-manager government in the eyes of citizens. In large measure, this legitimacy results from the public debates that accompany structural reform. Public debate grounds the reform in a community's political values and functions to make the structure conform to those values. The structure, then, is intermittently tested for its viability: Does it work the way the citizens want it to work?

In contrast to this public debate are discussions that take place within the profession over the roles, responsibilities, and values of city managers. These debates occur frequently among self-reflective city managers, the stimulus being the International City Management Code of Ethics and Declaration of Ideals. No matter how open this dialogue, however, it occurs within the profession, within "the community of competence." It is probably reasonable to suggest that even the most politically enlightened citizens have virtually no idea about the self-reflection that goes on in city management circles.

I see a pronounced difference between the legitimacy for the structure of local governments that adapt publicly to change and the credibility of the city management profession itself. The profession has adapted equally well but is saddled with a public orthodoxy that does not reflect the transformations that have occurred in the role, responsibilities, and values of city managers.

The transformation in the basic tenets of city management reflect the desire of the city management profession to practice its craft effectively within the context of contemporary representative democracy. But the tenets have not been crystallized and concisely articulated publicly. Further, they stand in contrast to the orthodox view of city management, as outlined in Chapter One, and espoused by community leaders and in authoritative documents.

For example, the *Kansas City Times,* in an editorial entitled "The Svehla Appointment" (1989), defended city management with the following argument: "The charter, however, is clear. Policy is established by the council, which is to be carried out by the city manager, his department heads and others in the administration." Similarly, in northern California, Wesley McClure, long-time city manager now retired and working for the League of California Municipalities, is reported to have described the council-manager plan as follows: "The whole concept of the council-manager form is that the council makes policy and the manager carries it out" (Cabanatuan, 1988).

As another example, the City of Dallas publishes a brochure (undated publication no. 84-85-58), "The Key to the City: Council-Manager Government in Dallas," which explains council-manager government this way: "The City of Dallas organization under the council-manager plan is similar to that of a corporation. The mayor and city council, as elected officers for the city, serve as the equivalent of a board of directors. They set the overall policy guidelines and appoint the city manager who acts as chief executive, seeing that the city operates in keeping with the council's guidelines."

The Dallas brochure and the newspaper descriptions of the council-manager plan are based on formal pronouncements and are not wrong; they simply do not do a very good job of capturing the tension and dynamism in modern city management. Despite the behavioral and structural changes that have occurred in city management over the years, the pictures drawn of the plan for today's citizens often are no different from what one might have seen fifty to seventy-five years ago.

The remaining chapters attempt to bring to light the transformations that have taken place in the roles, responsibilities, and values of city managers as a complement to the structural changes. The discussion is organized around three tenets, each of which challenges a component of the orthodox view.

Part Two

BUILDING A
CONTEMPORARY
FOUNDATION
FOR PROFESSIONALISM

4

Understanding the
Contemporary Role
of the City Manager

The orthodox view of council-manager government is dated but resilient as it fits council-manager government nicely into the normative precepts of representative democracy. Yet beneath the orthodoxy is a practical world of political pressures and tensions. In the previous chapter the structural responses to these political challenges were identified and discussed. The more direct challenge to city management may be the growing distance between the orthodox view and the transformations that have taken place over several years in the roles, responsibilities, and values of local government professionals. In fact, as the structural characteristics of council-manager and strong-mayor government begin to blend (Adrian, 1988; Renner, 1988; Anderson, 1989), the essence of the local government manager's professionalism may be found more in a commitment to certain roles, responsibilities, and values than in the design features discussed in Chapter Three. This chapter is the first to explore a set of tenets designed to replace the orthodox view that

Note: Parts of this chapter have appeared in "The Tenets of Contemporary Professionalism in Local Government," *Public Administration Review,* 1990, *50,* 654–662; and "The Contemporary Role of the City Manager," *American Review of Public Administration,* 1989, *19,* 261–278.

politics and administration are separate spheres of action, that the manager's role is legitimated in accountability to the governing body, and that efficiency—rational, analytical problem solving—can lead to a determination of "what is good for the city."

I have tried to formulate a set of tenets that bring together city management practice—"what it is"—and normative theory—"what it ought to be." This chapter focuses on the first of the following three tenets.

Three Tenets of Professionalism

I. Roles

Policy-making and administration are shared functions of government even though distinctions may prevail. While council-manager government may distinguish between the administrative authority of the city manager and the policy-making authority of the governing body, traditionalists have extended these distinctions into role expectations as well. This extension has created the impression that the role of the city manager as policymaker and as a broker and negotiator of community interests and power is somehow illegitimate.

II. Responsibility

The local government professional is formally accountable to the governing body. But as the manager's role extends into policy-making and the negotiating and brokering of community interests and power, more than council approval for the role is required. The more political responsibility the governing body shares with the manager, the greater the need to extend the city manager's traditional commitment to accountability into a framework at city hall that engages professionalism with value diversity in the community. The successful manager's role is grounded in the authority of the governing body and in the trust and approval of those who will be affected by the manager's influence.

III. Values

The value of efficiency still underpins the local government management profession, bringing with it the application of knowledge and expertise to local government problems. But efficiency by itself inadequately describes the value base of professionalism in contemporary local management. Representation, individual rights, and social equity frequently compete with efficiency and have forced upon managers concerns for the authoritative foundations of public policy processes and substance.

The first tenet acknowledges shared functions of governance. Managers are involved in the political side of things, and political values have penetrated administrative processes.

The City Manager's Involvement in Politics

Svara (1985, 1990), among others, has probed rethinking about professionalism in modern city management, suggesting an alternative to the dichotomy model. Svara's research led him to propose a model of shared values, responsibility, and cooperative roles, eschewing the means/ends dichotomy and separated role expectations between elected and appointed officials. He divides governance into four functions: mission, policy, administration, and management. The dichotomy model would predict a dominant role for the governing body in the mission and policy arenas, with city managers fulfilling the administration and management functions. In fact, as scholars (Stone, Price, and Stone, 1940; Bollens and Ries, 1969; Stillman, 1974; Newell and Ammons, 1987) and practitioners have acknowledged for years, the lines blur, with managers playing significant roles in the mission and policy functions while political values influence administrative processes.

While city managers always have played important roles in the policy-making arena, the nature of contemporary political, economic, and social forces in local government appears to have encouraged the negotiating, brokerage, and consensus-building skills of today's managers more than among early predecessors (Green, 1987; Hale, 1989; Hinton and Kerrigan, 1989; Rutter, 1980; Stillman, 1974).

When cities were building sewers and streets, city managers were recruited from the ranks of civil engineers. Today's managers are very different from their engineering predecessors because the political attention in today's communities has changed. Revenue shortfalls, special-interest politics, intergovernmental relations, mass media coverage, and demographic shifts have altered the dynamics of contemporary local government and the role expectations of local government professionals.

Managers themselves acknowledge the changes. Mark Keane (1987, p. 103), former executive director of the ICMA says:

> The old concept of the council-manager plan, where everyone on the council would represent city wide interests, and would be immune from special interest pressures, is much less of a practical concept today than it once was. So the manager now is thrust more often into the role of negotiator and mediator. . . . The political role of the manager now is more important and difficult.

Walter Scheiber (1987, p. 195), executive director of the Metropolitan Washington Council of Governments, reinforces Keane's remarks:

> Here in the Washington area, for example, on some of the tough intergovernmental issues the elected officials quietly say to the managers, "Negotiate that problem with those other three governments. When you get a solution, bring it back to me. If I like it—and I probably will—then we'll have a ceremony and a press conference, and I'll sign a document. It will be mine, but we'll all know that you did it."
>
> Twenty years ago that would have been unthinkable. The managers would have stayed out of policy. They would not have negotiated with their peers. This may become a pattern across the country in which the managers, who, after all, have the information, are prime negotiators as well as managers, and the elected officials deal with other kinds of policy questions.

Recent articles by Kirchoff (1990) and to a lesser extent by Griesemer (1990) would lead one to believe that managers have chosen to become involved in policy-making and community politics. To the contrary, role theory (Katz and Kahn, 1978) would suggest that role definitions are developed largely from one's own personality as well as from the expectations of others rather than from a formal job description and deliberate choices managers make about what they are going to do as city managers. The expectations of councils, department heads and professional staff, peers, and citizens seeking access to levers of power have considerable influence over the role the manager must fulfill in order to be successful.

Howard Tipton (1989, p. 178), city manager in Daytona Beach, provides a glimpse of the problems and activities a city manager faces in a dynamic economic environment:

> soliciting proposals for a new convention center and headquarters hotel; negotiating for parking that will help existing business; working to secure a new anchor tenant for downtown; selling the need for a new harbor development that creates a drawing for redevelopment areas; negotiating for new city golf courses so as to improve community recreation and attract high quality residential development; convincing a developer to provide a free site for a new stadium and selling the old stadium site to a university for its expansion needs; packaging a low interest loan program with local bankers to facilitate the rehabilitation of downtown buildings; negotiating the purchase of key sites that accomplish redevelopment needs; negotiating with property owners outside the city to annex their property; negotiating interlocal agreements among local governments for provision of services or distribution of revenues; and lobbying state legislators.

Meeting the challenges in Tipton's list requires substantial technical expertise. Moreover, the expertise extends to an understanding of the political, economic, and social dimensions of these challenges. Further, to be effective, the city manager must at times balance the expectations that the governing body has of the manager with the expectations of an increasingly professionalized staff. Successful contemporary city managers approach their work with a high level of managerial skill, problem-solving ability, interpersonal sensitivity, tolerance for ambiguity, and willingness to accept responsibility.

The Manager As Policymaker

The issues that managers bring before councils, the information they present to support their recommendations, and the directions they provide to employees to carry out public policy all involve the manager in the policy-making process. Tipton's activities, listed earlier, provide concrete examples of managerial discretion and the influence many managers have in public policy-making.

Importance of the Policy-making Role. In 1985 Newell and Ammons (1987) surveyed 527 chief executive officers in local governments to determine how they divided their time between political, policy, and management activities, and to determine which area the executives identified as most important to their work. They compared the results to a similar survey conducted in 1965 (Wright, cited in Newell and Ammons, 1987, p. 252). In both studies, the chief executive officer's political role included relationships with nongovernmental groups and individuals within the city, as well as with intergovernmental actors; the policy role centered on council agenda and policy initiation and formulation; and the management role included activities like staffing, budgeting, and supervision. In the 1985 study, council relations was added to the policy role. The comparison of results in Table 3 shows a considerable increase between 1965 and 1985 in the percent of managers citing the policy-making role as most important.

Svara (1988) surveyed 189 North Carolina city and county managers in 1987 and 1988 to determine the amount of time they spent in the areas of mission, policy, administration, and management in comparison with their estimate of the amount of time council members spent on these activities. His results show that managers consistently rate themselves as more involved in *all* four

Table 3. Role Importance for City Managers (Percent).

	Importance	
Role	1985	1965
Management	39	37
Policy	56	22
Political	6	33
	N = 52	N = 45

Sources: Newell and Ammons (1987) and Wright (cited in Newell and Ammons). Newell and Ammons note that Wright's figures do not equal 100 percent.

areas of local government decision making when compared to their councils. City size has no effect on this finding.

In another part of his survey, Svara asked managers to respond to a series of statements about policy-related activities. The results confirm his other findings. Eighty percent of the respondents agreed that the manager should "assume leadership in shaping municipal policies." However, his results here are somewhat ambivalent, as suggested by the 52 percent of the respondents who agreed with the statement, "A manager should act as an administrator and leave policy matters to the council."

The ICMA conducted surveys in 1973 (Huntley and Macdonald, 1975) and in 1984 (Green, 1987), permitting a comparison of policy-related activities of managers over time. In 1973, 1,687 city managers and chief administrative officers were asked how often they participate in the formulation of municipal policy, play a leading role in policy-making, and initiate municipal policies.

The results, shown in Table 4, suggest substantial involvement of managers in the policy-making process, including the initiation of public policy. The results in the 1984 survey (not shown) of 2,384 respondents were virtually identical.

Council Expectations. In these two ICMA surveys (Huntley and Macdonald, 1975; Green, 1987), managers were also asked about council expectations of the city manager. Respondents were given six expectations to choose from:

Table 4. City Manager Involvement in Policy-making, 1973.

Activity	Mean
Participate in policy formulation	1.5
Play a leading role in policy-making	2.3
Initiate municipal policies	2.3
1 = "always"; 5 = "never."	

Source: Huntley and Macdonald (1975).

- exercise political leadership
- exercise administrative leadership
- advise council
- participate in issue formulation
- develop objectives, strategies
- other

While managers in both surveys identified the "exercise of administrative leadership" as the council's primary expectation, the results showed a decrease from 83 percent in 1973 to 61 percent in 1984. Moreover, in 1973 only 8 percent selected "participation in issue formulation" as the best description of the council's expectations, whereas in 1984 that figure jumped to 25 percent.

Managers Fill a Policy Void. The increasing participation of managers in the policy-making process is due only in part to the nature of contemporary politics, which brings so many difficult issues to public forums. In addition, it can be attributed to policy voids left by the governing body, the manager's own predisposition to "be in charge," and in many instances the governing body's own expectations (Svara, 1990).

Surveys of council members (National League of Cities, 1980) and managers (Svara, 1988) support the view that councils are not very effective policy-making bodies. For example, according to Svara's research, more managers, 30 percent, rated their councils "poor" in policy-making compared to the 20 percent who rated them high. Similarly, in the National League of Cities survey, when asked to assess the effectiveness of the various functions the council performs, only 50 percent indicated the council is "very or usually effective" when "setting long-term goals." This contrasts with 93 percent of the council members who responded that the council is "very effective" or "usually effective" when responding to citizen needs.

Managers in Charge. Research also suggests that managers are administrative leaders who take special pride in seeing the results of their work. Thus, their own personal desire to feel worthwhile may lead them to fill a policy-making void left by their governing body.

In 1983 Schilling (1989), a former city manager, presented 213 California city managers with a list of eighteen management values—terms like "rationality," "idealism," "accountability," and "practicality." He asked respondents to rank the eighteen values in order of importance. Of the eighteen, "administrative leadership" was first. These results correspond with a similar survey conducted by Nalbandian and Edwards (1983; Edwards, Nalbandian, and Wedel, 1981) in the late 1970s, comparing the professional values of M.B.A. and M.P.A. students and alumni. Athough the business and government students and alumni differed noticeably on their ranking of the values "efficiency" and the "public interest," both groups selected "leadership" as one of the highest values. And last, in the ICMA "1988 State of the Profession Survey Results" (International City Management Association, 1988), when asked to identify "the two most important factors in your decision to remain in the local government management profession," the two top factors were "commitment to public service" (77 percent) and "desire to be in charge" (26 percent). John Dever (1987), city manager in Long Beach, California, expresses the manager's motivation this way: "He or she must be willing to come out at the top of a pack of three or four and actually *want* to lead. In fact, he or she must be willing to knock down the other three because of a commitment and desire to lead. It is not good enough to simply let things take their natural course. . . . That attitude isn't going to solve the city's problems or set the stage so that Hispanic kids, for example, can finally learn English or get a job" (p. 18).

The Manager As Broker of Community Power

"Welcome, I am Jennifer Stene, the city coordinator . . . The job of 'coordinator' is similar to the job of a

city manager or administrator twenty years ago," she
explains. "Names change over the years, but the job
is very much the same." One of the few differences is
that as coordinator, she spends most of her time with
the council and community leaders. She is the broker
among the various political and social groups in
town, and her assistant actually manages the community on a day-to-day basis [Rutter, 1980, p. 2].

Jennifer Stene's job description originated with the ICMA's
Future Horizons Committee, chaired by George Schrader, former
city manager of Dallas and former president of the ICMA. That
committee set its sights on describing what city management would
be like in the year 2000. It identified the prime role of the manager
as that of broker or negotiator. Ten years after *The Essential Community* (Rutter, 1980), the job description appears unmistakenly
accurate.

Recent research (Hinton and Kerrigan, 1989; Hale, 1989)
reinforces the view that a significant dimension of the manager's
job involves coordinating/negotiating and brokerage. In 1987–1988
Hinton and Kerrigan surveyed 478 city managers who had received
"service award recognition" from the ICMA. Their goal was to
identify the knowledge and skills most important for city managers
and to compare the results with similar surveys conducted in 1978–
1979 and even earlier in 1971. The managers were asked to rate the
salience of twelve skill areas for tomorrow's city managers on a 1
to 3 scale, with 1 being least important and 3 being most important.
The results showed remarkable stability over the two decades and
reinforced the idea that managers are and have been heavily involved in coordinating/brokering/negotiating community interests. Managers clearly indicate that skills identified with external
organizational relations are more important than those connected
to the technical side of administration. In the 1987–1988 survey the
four most important skills were

• Situational analysis; that is, "sizing up" the community political milieu, organization, and staff
• Assessing community needs

- Handling interpersonal relations
- Bargaining, negotiating, and other consensus-seeking techniques

"Bargaining, negotiating, and other consensus-seeking techniques" was identified as seventh most important in 1978–1979, and second in 1971. The average level of importance was 2.59, 2.53, and 2.54 in the three survey periods.

Least important skills for all three survey periods were those connected closely to nuts-and-bolts administrative aspects of the manager's job:

- Systems design and operations analysis
- Job analysis; that is, assessing the requirements and responsibilities of positions
- Organizing and writing policy statements, reports, etc.

Hale (1989) analyzed the nature of the city manager's work through direct observation. She spent 239 hours observing the work of five city managers in Los Angeles County in 1983. She distilled the manager's activities into five categories: broker, information agent, administrator, miscellaneous, and time the manager spent on solitary activities like reading or writing. Then she sorted the number of contacts into these categories and calculated the percentage of time spent in each role.

Her most important finding, presented in Table 5, is that 78 percent of the manager's time is spent in contact with someone; only 22 percent of the manager's time is spent on solitary activity like reading and paperwork. The results show that the broker category accounts for 37 percent of the manager's time. Hale (1989) observed, "In their role as brokers, city managers spent most of their time sharing knowledge, educating, negotiating or brokering among various groups, and instigating communication by linking people" (p. 174).

Over 2,000 members responded to a 1984 survey (Green, 1987) conducted by the ICMA. One question inquired into the amount of time managers spent on various activities. "Acting as negotiator to work out problems, resolve conflicts, and develop compromises" was the second most time-consuming activity, occupying an average

Table 5. City Manager Roles
and Amount of Contact with Others.

Role	Percent Time
Broker	37
Time Spent Alone	22
Information Agent	21
Administrator	15
Miscellaneous	5

N = 5 managers and 239 hours of observation

Source: Hale (1989) and communication between Hale and Nalbandian.

of 13 percent of the manager's time, just behind crisis management. Forty-one percent of the manager's time is spent in various activities that involve external organizational relations, and 31 percent on activities like hiring, assigning work, training staff, and allocating resources. An ICMA survey conducted in 1980 (Stillman, 1982) also produced results projecting the importance of brokerage skills for the future city manager.

Svara (1989a) addresses the qualifications of the manager to broker community interests by suggesting that as communities move to district elections and as the mayor's job becomes more difficult, the city manager may be the only one perceived to be interested in citywide concerns. Schmidt and Posner's research (1987) adds an element to the manager's qualifications to serve citywide interests. They compared responses of 238 city managers with those of executives in the federal service and private-sector executives whom they had questioned earlier. They surveyed "beliefs about what will improve the quality of life in our country," and found that 42 percent of the city managers cited "a value system emphasizing cooperation and improvement; an improvement of total human community," compared to 27 percent for the federal executives and only 19 percent for the private-sector executives who favored, by a large margin, "return to values emphasizing individual initiative and responsibility" (1987, p. 409).

The Role of Politics in Administration

If the changing context of municipal management has led to more visible roles for managers in the mission and policy functions of government and has enhanced their role as community leaders, it also has created opportunities for more political involvement in internal administrative activities. In other words, the manager's involvement in the spheres of community politics and policy-making is matched by the presence of political values in the administrative arena. Few local government professionals welcome political interest in administration and management when it affects established work plans and administrative procedure. Yet, often overlooked is the way political values have significantly penetrated administrative processes. Administrative processes have become systematically responsive to a variety of community and political interests, even as managers resist ad hoc interference from elected leaders and citizens.

Sharp (1986) and Thomas (1986) document neighborhood involvement in governance in Kansas City and Cincinnati. Both show an evolution in citizen participation from the 1960s, when the federal government mandated "maximum feasible participation" in public programs, to the 1980s, where citizen involvement through formal organizations, task forces, boards, and commissions has penetrated governing processes that formerly were seen as the exclusive domain of administrative staff.

Thomas (1986, chap. 7) characterizes the change in citizen participation as moving from "petition to negotiation" and from involvement with political leadership to an association with professional staff. He documents an ongoing relationship of cooperation between neighborhood and city departments, not only in areas of service delivery but in establishing budgetary priorities as well.

Examples of political and community involvement in the administrative core of municipal government are replicated nationwide. They appear to be qualitatively different from the mandated involvement of the poor and minorities in social programs of earlier decades in that they are cooperative in nature, focus on administrative process and access, and affect core city services.

Michael Gleason (telephone conversation, Nov. 1989, and letter to the author, Jan. 1990), city manager in Eugene, Oregon, reports on a governing process that focuses community values on budgetary activities. In the classic council-manager plan, the staff prepares an executive budget which the manager submits to the council for review and approval. In Eugene, relevant portions of the manager's executive budget are routed through appropriate boards and commissions before they become the focus of a public hearing. Then, according to state law, the manager transmits the budget to a public committee appointed by the city council. The public body, which includes council members, reviews the budget and submits its recommendation to the city council, which holds another hearing. The city council may alter the recommended budget by no more than 10 percent.

Gleason indicates that in 1988, thirty-two meetings were required before the budget was adopted in Eugene. More staff time is spent on budget preparation because the members of the public committee are not as knowledgeable as the council members and need to be presented with material they can understand. At the same time, staff worksheets are developed in more detail in anticipation of questions about individual line items where council members familiar with the budget process might simply defer to staff. Gleason returns to the budget committee and city council quarterly to reconcile the estimated budget with the actual budget.

The operation of some fifty-five boards and commissions involving some 500 citizens in Eugene also provides examples of how administrative aspects of government are increasingly influenced by citizen involvement. According to Gleason, the policy guidelines set by the city council say that it is the manager's formal responsibility to promulgate rules, regulations, and fees involving the airport. In practice, however, the staff develops administrative proposals that it forwards to the airport commission for review. The commission then recommends the proposal to the city manager, who authorizes a public hearing and then authorizes the rule or regulation. In effect, the airport commission becomes advisory to administrative staff, as well as being a channel for policy and budgetary proposals that will be brought before the city council.

The advisory role of the boards and commissions places a significant number of citizens in an intermediate position between their private lives and elected politics. The boards and commissions become a training ground for future council members. Further, the city council demonstrates sensitivity to the values of representation and social equity in its appointments. In fact, Gleason points out that the city maintains a personnel system that focuses on the demographic characteristics of the boards and commissions and includes a training program for new appointees.

The pervasive role of these boards and commissions has not only affected the administrative work of staff; it has also influenced the criteria used to make staff appointments. According to Gleason, it is essential that department heads are able and willing to work with these boards and commissions and neighborhood groups. Gleason recruits and selects department heads with this orientation in mind and then evaluates their work with these groups. Further, he does not staff these boards and commissions with junior employees.

Local government professionals appear highly cognizant of and sensitive to the impact of citizen participation and the political value of representation on administrative processes (Streib, 1990). Not to be neglected is the impact of individual rights, another political value, on administrative processes (Rosenbloom, 1987).

The influence of individual rights on personnel management, a core administrative function, is illustrated in the volatile area of drug testing today, where local governments take cues from the United States Supreme Court. In *National Treasury Employees Union* v. *von Raab* (1989) the Court reasoned (5-4) that the administrative process employed to test customs officers for drug and alcohol abuse so fully acknowledged their individual rights that the need for a search warrant, on its face guaranteed by the Fourth Amendment, would serve no purpose. In other words, in the Court's eyes it appears that the Customs Service had sufficiently incorporated the rights of its employees into the design of administrative processes that constitutional protection through the judicial system would be superfluous.

Similar injection of judicial values into administrative processes occurs in local government drug-testing programs, law enforcement, and wherever else administrative due process tempers the desire for economy and efficiency. This complex connection between individual rights and administrative processes occurs so commonly and has been accepted so readily that its significance in broadening the value base of administrative practice is easily taken for granted. The tempering of efficiency with such political values as representation and individual rights strengthens the legitimacy of administrative processes and the exercise of administrative discretion and reinforces the integrated character of politics and administration in practical governance (Rosenbloom, 1987).

Conclusions

While the concept of shared responsibility is easily recognized in the policy-making and brokerage activities of the manager, the way political values have steadily increased their influence over administrative processes is often unrecognized. Some observers (Newland, 1985; Svara, 1990) assert that the shared responsibility and the cooperation envisioned in council-manager government go hand in hand. However, shared values are hard to find among council members and between the governing body and staff in diverse and larger communities like Dallas, Kansas City, Fort Worth, and San Diego. Moreover, comments by managers about fragmented councils, political distrust of administrators, and the high stakes of special-interest politics are not uncommon (Nalbandian and Davis, 1987).

While a unification of powers encourages shared authority, more fundamental forces may be at work. First, for decades we have seen a rising trend toward reliance on expertise in public-policy formulation. There is no foreseeable end to this dependence, which necessitates more involvement of administrative staff in politics. Second, the disaffection and suspicion of government for the past two decades have placed a greater burden on all aspects of government, including the administrative and management functions, to earn the public's trust. This has forced the opening of administrative processes to political values, like representation, social equity, and individual rights, in a way that preserves administrative routine yet makes administrative process accessible to public scrutiny. Further, the "meddling" of council members in all functions of local government may simply reflect a time when citizens demand more visible evidence that their elected officials at all levels of government are "governing." Managers commonly assume that once elected to office, without any training and little orientation, citizens will know what policy is, will be skilled in coalition building, and will know the value of professional staff and the importance of respecting their autonomy.

While the movement toward overlapping roles and responsibility seems firmly entrenched, some research suggests trouble spots on the horizon, particularly in the area of managerial involvement in policy-making and community leadership. The caution centers on the decline of political leadership and the accompanying lack of respect that managers might develop for governing bodies. Svara's work (1989c) shows that while managers in Ohio prefer more involvement of elected officials in determining mission and policy, the average degree of involvement they desire for elected officials falls short of the manager's actual involvement. North Carolina managers also prefer more involvement of elected officials in mission and policy determination. But like Ohio managers, the average degree of involvement they prefer for elected officials in the policy area is less than the actual involvement managers report for themselves. It is only slightly greater than the manager's actual involvement in mission determination. While Svara (1985, p. 228) very cogently argues in favor of a "partnership model" of governance between council and manager, with the council acting as senior partner, managers consistently report more involvement in mission and policy areas—both in terms of actual and preferred levels—than his ideal model would appear to permit (Svara, 1989c).

Schilling's work (1989) also raises a flag of concern regarding the respect that managers have for elected leaders and the political process. Schilling asked managers to rank eighteen values that they believed were most important in the practice of municipal administration. He reports that managers ranked "administrative leadership" as the most important value and "political leadership," defined on the questionnaire as "effective elected officials," last (p. 145).

These results from Svara and Schilling's work are troublesome if the policy-active and brokerage roles are not accompanied by more discussion of their implications for the accountability of managers. Also, their results should stimulate discussion of the values that establish the context for contemporary professionalism. While the partnership model of governance insightfully describes the relationship between politics and administration, the vague boundaries raise questions about oversight and accountability (Gruber, 1987; Lowi, 1979; Mosher, 1982; Redford, 1969). To address the connection between accountability and the discretion of the professional manager, a second tenet of contemporary professionalism in local government requires analysis.

5

Accountability:
Broadening the Contemporary
City Manager's
Base of Legitimacy

The tradition of city management includes a commitment to accountability which takes new forms and is expressed in new terms as political conditions change. The espoused orthodox theory of city management describes the manager as a politically neutral administration expert. With this theory it makes sense to draw crisp lines of accountability; the manager is accountable to a governing body that, in turn, is responsible to the people. In this classic form, democratic values and accountability are upheld—the governing body makes policy and the manager, serving at the pleasure of the governing body, carries it out.

In practice, however, as power in communities has dispersed and citizens demand more and more access to government decision making, managers have become actively involved in policy-making processes and the negotiation and brokering of community interests. As the political power and discretion of the manager and pro-

Note: Parts of this chapter appeared in "The Contemporary Role of the City Manager," *American Review of Public Administration*, 1989, *19*, 261–278.

fessional staff are scrutinized, professional managers frequently find that "giving an account" to the governing body alone provides insufficient credibility for their visible and powerful role (Cooper, 1991; Lane and Wolf, 1990).

To broaden the base of legitimacy for their expanding role, managers frequently find themselves developing constituencies— incidentally and, on occasion, purposefully—beyond those represented clearly in the governing body (Ehrenhalt, 1990; Wamsley and others, 1987). A circular process operates where, in theory, the manager provides access, develops constituents who have influenced the manager and benefited from the access, and thereby may enhance his or her role as manager. This process constitutes an informal mechanism of accountability. The citizens can use the access to influence the manager, the manager's role is enhanced, but citizens are in a position to question the manager's role with reports to the governing body.

Tenet II attempts to answer the question, "How is it possible to share responsibility for policy-making and community building between the governing body and the city manager and still maintain accountability of the city manager to elected officials and democratic values?"

Tenet II

The local government professional is formally accountable to the governing body. But as the manager's role extends into policy-making and the negotiating and brokering of community interests and power, more than council approval for the role is required. The more political responsibility the governing body shares with the manager, the greater the need to extend the city manager's traditional commitment to accountability into a framework at city hall that engages professionalism with value diversity in the community. The successful manager's role is grounded in the authority of the governing body and in the trust and approval of those who will be affected by the manager's influence.

This chapter gives voice to managers who are addressing issues of accountability. Their words reflect the profession's traditional acceptance of accountability to the city council and also a broader commitment to doing what is best for the city (Gruber, 1987; Hall-Saltzstein, 1985). But they also reflect the struggle that managers face as they attempt to balance these traditional legal and idealist notions of accountability with pressures to legitimize their contemporary role by responding to political constituencies, community interests, and values. Weighing these forces may challenge the governing body's authority and the manager's own sense of professionalism.

Formal and Idealist Traditions of Accountability

The respect that contemporary managers show for the governing body is enforced most practically by a formal superior-subordinate employment relationship. But it is also reflected in various themes derived from acceptance of the value of political supremacy in council-manager government. Underlying the ideal of the manager who answers to democratic values and serves the city as a whole is the notion that city management is a calling.

According to Bellah and his coauthors (1985, p. 88), an occupation is a calling when "defined essentially in terms of its contribution to the public good" instead of personal advancement. To the extent that city management is a calling, managers are called to public service. Bellah continues: "We need to reappropriate the ethical meaning of professionalism, seeing it in terms not only of technical skill but of the moral contributions that professionals make to a complex society. . . . To change the conception of government from scientific management to a center of ethical obligations and relationships is part of our task" (p. 211).

Nalbandian and Edwards (1983) found that, early in their graduate education or in their career, city managers realize they want to work in local government, they want to be in charge, and they want to make a difference in pursuit of the public interest. The results of ICMA's State of the Profession Surveys consistently show "commitment to public service" as a primary reason city managers enter their profession.

The idea of city management as a calling is not new. Charles E. Ashburner, generally recognized as the first city manager, said to his colleagues at the first national meeting of the City Managers' Association in 1914: "The question of managing cities is a very important one, and one in which a man must have a sincere feeling of wishing to do something for the permanent good of mankind or else no man with sufficient ability to make good in life could be induced to stay long enough in the game to really get interested" (City Managers' Association, 1914, p. 4).

Tom Downs (1987), chief administrative officer in the District of Columbia and former city manager, provides contemporary comment on this idealistic side of city management: "You are there to do things for the public good, and that purpose sets the context for the values and styles that you bring to government. You are there to serve it, not it you. You are there, I hope, with a sense of humility about the process of handling the levers of government. At times, the decisions are awesome in their complexity. You have to approach them with a sense of assurance about your own skills and with a sense of humility about where you fit in the larger piece of machinery. Then you hope that your effort makes the whole thing work better" (p. 26). Robert Kipp (1987) adds: "I think we all need to be reminded and to remind ourselves about democracy. Without that framework, we're adrift. As city managers, we are agents to make the experiment of democracy work at the local level" (p. 112).

Accountability in Practice

Managers work hard to bring together their legal obligations to the governing body and their professional obligations to serve the public's interest as a whole. They employ a number of explanations for their behavior which permit us to observe the way they attempt to hold themselves accountable. Several of the explanations reflect sophisticated reasoning as managers attempt to engage the demands for accountability with the challenges of the manager's expanding role.

First, managers suggest that their negotiating and brokering activities are justified as long as the council is kept abreast of the manager's activities and accepts ultimate responsibility for public policy decisions. Second, according to city managers, their policy-related activities should take place behind the scenes in order to maintain the community's political focus on the council—where it belongs. Third, managers act in some relationship to the council, either by following the broad guidelines established by the council or by filling a void that council inaction creates. Last, managers believe that policy-making is not politics; it is problem solving.

Council Authority for Policy Decisions. For all managers, at various levels of sophisticated understanding, the ultimate justification for whatever they do is that the governing body has the final say. In 1969, upon his retirement after forty years in public service and twenty-five as a city manager, Carleton F. Sharpe (1969) wrote: "In submitting such [policy] recommendations, the manager is involved in policy formulation. But the policy *decision* in every case is exclusively vested in the elected council. It is the final decision that determines the policy, and not the process which precedes such final action" (p. 407). Some two decades later, David Mora (1987), city manager in Oxnard, California, reiterates the view that the council is the final authority: "Elected officials are much more involved and much more demanding than formerly. . . . It is frustrating at times, because although I do say they know the community, I'm still saying I am the expert. It has led to some clashes, but in the final analysis they are right" (pp. 125–126).

Part of the manager's deference to the governing body includes the manager's sensitivity about moving too far ahead of the council. Curtis Branscome, city manager in Decatur, Georgia, and former ICMA president says: "When I wake up in the middle of the night thinking about my job it's invariably because I wonder if I have gone too far this time without touching base with the council. . . . For example, I thought I might have gone too far when I was pursuing a general mandate from the council to get a conference center/hotel/parking complex built in a public/private partnership. I remember negotiating prices and costs which could ultimately come back to affect the council members at election time. I felt like I was really out on a limb, and I quickly went back to the governing body for a reality check, and I got a resolution passed so they knew what I was doing" (personal interview, Apr. 1989).

Regardless of what city managers do and what they know, they are formally accountable to their councils. In the manager's eyes, this is the fail-safe mechanism that guards against the unwarranted exercise of managerial influence and discretion.

Behind the Scenes. In an interview in 1986 Robert Herchert (1986), city manager in Fort Worth, said: "It is the nature of democracy for elected officials to take the limelight. In fact, that is often an important reason why people run for office. Managers should participate in policy-making behind the scenes and indirectly." Managers play to this theme continuously. Robert Kipp (1987) tells the story of the city manager who asks the taxi driver in the town he or she is visiting who the city manager is. If the cab driver knows, there is something out of the ordinary in the relationship between the manager and the council, with the manager receiving too much media attention. Kipp was recognized by his peers with election to the presidency of the ICMA, and in many circles he was considered the prototype city manager. He dislikes giving speeches, for example, and during a particularly antagonistic strike between the firefighters and the city in 1980, he was critical of the mayor for not taking a more public role, forcing Kipp into the political arena as the focal point of the media.

To take the spotlight and the credit away from the governing body is inappropriate and in some instances considered unethical, according to the Code of Ethics of the ICMA (1984). The Sixth Tenet of the code states that the manager should "Recognize that elected representatives of the people are entitled to the credit for the establishment of municipal policies; responsibility for policy execution rests with the members."

On the other hand, councils expect the manager to accept blame generously for a failed policy, and in so doing, possibly relieve some pressure from a failed council decision or nondecision. Tom Lewinsohn (conversations with the author, 1987), personnel director in Kansas City, Missouri, and a former president of the International Personnel Management Association, tells the story of a council member's complaint about the city manager. The city council faced a decision made to satisfy political considerations that the members knew ran against the long-run interests of the city. The council member expressed surprise at the manager, whom she had expected to advocate more strongly the professional recommendation. His advocacy would have allowed the council to follow his recommendation and cushion the council's political vulnerability, shifting blame for the decision to professional staff, who are usually buffered from the quickly changing winds of public opinion.

Following Council Guidance or Filling a Policy-making Void. Managers would agree with Svara (1989c), that the political context shapes their latitude in policy-making. If the council desires a policy-active role for the manager, the manager is likely to respond. The opposite is probably equally true; where the council wants the manager to concentrate on administrative matters, the manager is likely to comply—although with varying degrees of satisfaction. The difficulty comes where the council is willing but unable to fulfill its policy-making role or when it simply abdicates the responsibility. In either of these cases, there is a policy void that will affect the ability of the city manager to effectively carry out administrative functions and provide guidance for staff. Tipton (1989) describes this kind of scenario: "Managers recommend policy on a regular basis and council members initiate policy. The experience and knowledge of the manager afford the council the expertise to recommend answers for the great majority of issues that come before them. *Council members, as elected officials, are by nature problem avoiders* [emphasis added]. The manager can make the hard choices between competing interests in the creation of policy and present the overall policy to the council for final approval" (p. 177).

Nathan's newspaper report (Mar. 8, 1989) about Arlington, Texas, reinforces Tipton's view. He writes, "The City Council passed the buck to City Manager William Kirchoff on Tuesday on a proposal to cut a projected deficit by eliminating 24 city positions, giving him no advice except to make the decision on his own."

Larry Brown contrasts the political context he faced in Arlington County, Virginia, and Hillsborough County, Florida. In Arlington, "The community knew precisely what it wanted to do, knew precisely where it was going, and wouldn't tolerate any major deviations from that clearly marked path. With such a consensus public policy, my role in Arlington was more of an authoritative stabilizer as we moved toward that common goal" (Brown, 1989, p. 95). In contrast, he says there is little consensus in Hillsborough County, where the base of power has broadened in the past few decades and where there is about a 25 percent in- and out-migration annually. "In this situation, the professional manager must become a major player in policy development . . . doing as much as possible to put the community in a posture to lead itself—through facilitating, through identifying issues, through processing [the debate]" (p. 95).

Policy-making Is Problem Solving, Not Politics. Hale (1989) observes that the manager's "policy role is one of a group of invisible activities; that is, through information gathering and disseminating these managers [those in her research study] stimulate policy . . . [and] stimulate council members toward implementation of an overall plan" (p. 174). These invisible policy-making activities might elicit images of backroom decision making, but this is not the way managers describe their policy-making role. In fact, many see policy-making as nonpolitical. Eric Anderson (1989), city manager in Eau Claire, Wisconsin, expresses this view clearly: "I am a check on politics, leavening the policy process with objective, technical, managerial information and activity. Managers should not determine policy.* Yet without professional involvement, policy would lack objectivity and integration, as well as the technical and managerial basis needed for it to be effective. Managers are expected to be involved in policy formulation and advocacy. Most residents do not consider it a political role in the same way they define the political role of council members" (p. 195).

Anderson's reasoning is intricate. First, he distinguishes between "determining" public policy and "leavening" the policy process, with the former deemed inappropriate. Then he suggests that leavening (influencing) the policy process with objective, technical information, which has as its goal public policy "integration," is not political. The inference is that what politicians do is bring

*Based on my April 7, 1989, correspondence with Anderson, I have substituted "should not determine policy" for "cannot determine policy."

"representational" interests to the policy-making process, which is political because it involves trade-offs where short-term gains and special interests may dominate over longer-term integrated policy, informed by analysis.

Larry Brown (1989) reflects a similar view when he describes his involvement in policy development in Hillsborough County, Florida, where there is little policy consensus: "This [facilitating, processing, identifying issues by the manager] doesn't impose the professional manager's outcome. Rather, it defines the issues, sets an agenda and sets in motion a process whereby the community can come up with its own conclusions" (p. 95). Like Anderson, Brown suggests that "determining" or "imposing" policy outcomes is inappropriate. But defining issues and setting an agenda to promote a policy-making consensus is appropriate.

Brown continues: "The balancing act a professional manager performs in this politically charged arena [complex issues, single issue candidates, emphasis on citizen participation] is to manage the power of others without merging himself in the power base in a way that would challenge the elected governing body" (pp. 94–95).

Brown seems to be drawing a very fine yet clear line here between appropriate and inappropriate political involvement. Moreover, it would be a mistake to dismiss Brown's statement as idiosyncratic, as this comment by Charles Anderson (1986), city manager in Dallas, suggests: "The worst thing that could happen to a city manager is to become a caretaker or pawn of whatever community based groups happen to be powerful at the moment. *It takes a lot of vigilance and a lot of energy to stay neutral but influential*" [emphasis added].

The idea that the manager is objective and unbiased is a theme managers echo when talking about their exercise of power, whether it be in their brokering role or when more directly involved in public policy formulation with the governing body. Brown (1989) expresses this view very clearly: "In a political arena filled with elected officials who have their own constituencies and their own philosophies and values, there is a greater likelihood of arriving at an acceptable consensus with the help of a manager whose only desire is to do the best professional job possible" (p. 94). He elaborates: "A professional manager working in the political arena doesn't have to worry about accumulating political power for himself in order to do the job. He accepts the distribution of power as it exists and tries to accommodate the differences by keying in on common ground" (p. 94).

These statements by E. Anderson, Brown, and C. Anderson reveal an intricate pattern in the way managers think about their own roles and attempt to distinguish their exercise of power from the elected officials' exercise of power. Implied is the manager's recognition of and sensitivity to the challenge that the manager does act politically.

The Political Nature of Problem Solving

Problem solving is what managers say they do; it is what they enjoy doing and what frustrates them when they cannot do it well. In separate surveys of ICMA members in the 1980s, Green (1987) and Stillman (1982) both report that "seeing the results of their work" was the most satisfying aspect of city management to the managers responding to the surveys. Further, Stillman reports that compared to a similar survey conducted in the early 1970s, managers report more frustration in the 1980s with their ability to get things done.

The notion of city management as problem solving fits well with an orthodox view of the manager's role. Problem solving requires experts who exchange knowledge in a climate of cooperation and harmony. This picture permits managers to distinguish themselves conceptually from politicians and politics (Aberbach, Putnam, and Rockman, 1981). Politics is a game played by people who represent interests. It is fueled by the exchanges and exercise of power designed to bring about compromise in value conflicts.

While it is professionally useful for managers to characterize themselves as problem solvers, Ackoff (1979, p. 99) suggests that managers do not solve problems at all; rather, they deal with them, or in his words, "they manage messes." The metaphor of the problem as a mess is attractive because it suggests a more realistic approach to city management than a scientific management advocate would endorse.

As more people and interests define a problem, as the stakes of policy and regulatory decisions increase, and as governing bodies have shown reluctance to make policy decisions, managerial problem-solving skills have changed to keep pace. They are being supplemented with political skills. There is more brokering and negotiation going on than decision making because the clarity of goals and the concentrations of knowledge and power necessary for efficient problem solving are being replaced by dissensus in the community and on governing bodies, and by a diffusion of power.

According to Wamsley and others (1987), the political environment of contemporary public management requires that "the public administrator must engage not in a struggle for markets and profits, but in a contest with other actors in the political process for jurisdiction, legitimacy, and resources" (p. 300). They continue: "The uncertainty and complexity of modern-day governance demand not comprehensiveness but tentative strategies, social interaction, and frequent feedback and adjustment. From this perspective, not only is the postindustrialized administrative state compatible with involvement by citizens but it positively requires it" (pp. 313–314).

In this struggle, managers are and must be more connected than their predecessors to the politics and *all* the values in their communities because the values of representation, social equity, and individual rights are so politically salient today. These values and their advocates cannot be forced out of policy-making or even administrative thinking. This confounds the ideal that the manager can know and do "what is right for the city as a whole." Willbern (1984) writes, "The voice of the people will not be clear, it will not be based on full knowledge, it will conflict in small or large degree with other persuasive and powerful normative choices" (p. 106). The diversity of today's citizenry and the political implications of that diversity render the question "What is right for the city?" not only controversial, but in some cases, simply impossible to answer, objectively.

Sylvester Murray (1987), city manager in San Diego and past president of the ICMA, portrays a "problem solving as politics" view: "I have been accused of making policy or trying to make policy when I should have been just part of the administration. I have been accused of being a politician because I get out in the community. And I do make speeches, and I do talk to the citizens, and I do encourage neighborhood groups, and I do listen to them, and I do make the city bureaucracies change because a neighborhood group says that they want something. I think that I have been right all these years and that more is going to be demanded from managers who haven't been doing that" (p. 156).

I find Murray's words provocative because they contrast sharply with the view that "policy-making is not politics." The question managers face as they approach the year 2000 is whether or not they can continue to be involved in determining mission and policy and in the negotiation and brokering of community interests yet remain apart from community politics *as others see it and define the term.*

In light of an expanding role in mission determination and policy-making, demands for accountability and credibility may very well require more understanding by managers of the values that are being disputed in a community's politics (Gruber, 1987). This is why I suggest in Tenet II that managers will find themselves increasingly sensitive to the need to give an account of their work to those affected by it. This does not mean suffering a formal appraisal; it does mean refining the manager's sense of the political implications of his or her behavior for his or her own standing and weighing in the balance obligations to a broader set of democratic values.

Managers illustrate a problem solving as politics perspective even though they might not embrace it as a characterization of their work. For example, Michael Wildgen spent fifteen years as assistant city manager in Lawrence, Kansas, before being appointed manager in 1990. He appears nonpolitical and unassuming, and few would identify him as a political city manager. But when he meets with a representative of the Native American community, neighborhood residents, a nightclub owner, and his own police department to discuss points of contention, he finds himself unavoidably in the middle of community politics. His success in reaching an agreement among the parties builds for him a base of political support independent of the governing body, and it is likely that word of his success will get to individual council members. He did not intend to act politically, but he could not avoid it and do his job. The overlooked point is that in making himself accessible to these community interests, he also makes himself accountable to them. If he anticipates the will of the people in his actions, he is judged to have done well; if he fails to do so, he is judged to have overstepped the discretion of an appointed official.

Jan Hart, city manager in Dallas, finds herself in a politically charged environment in which she must name a new police chief. The police department is divided along racial lines. Anglo officers and police support groups assailed the former chief, an Anglo, as an outsider who advanced affirmative action at the expense of Anglo officers and who curried favor from minority politicians. In this context, traditional city manager theory suggests that Hart should make an objective choice. But can she? If she chooses an outsider—regardless of race—she will lose the rank-and-file Anglo officer. If she chooses an Anglo insider, she runs the risk of alienating support from the minority community and minority members of the governing body. If she chooses an African American insider, she will alienate the senior Anglo managers who would have been passed over. No matter what choice she makes, and no matter how nonpolitical she tries to make it, it will affect her ability to be successful in the future as the city manager of Dallas. Her decision will substantially affect those she works for, those who work for her, and the people of Dallas, who are struggling with racial disharmony. She cannot avoid the political overtones of her decision; those who are affected by the decision will make sure of it. Informally, she will be held accountable by the community and the officers in the police department, as well as formally by the governing body.

Camille Barnett finds herself further out on the political spectrum. Ehrenhalt (1990) characterizes Barnett's behavior as "performances any governor, any mayor, any congressman would find it difficult to improve on. The woman is a natural campaigner. What she is not, or at least is scrupulous not to appear to be, is a politician" (p. 41). Ehrenhalt, an astute observer of local government, recognizes that Barnett's behavior cannot be separated from her personality, but he goes on to suggest: "One would be hard-pressed to claim that the changing role of the city manager has been the catalyst for changing urban public policy. In general, the managers have been responding to the empowerment of new forces in the community, not creating it. Still, it would be fair to say that by acting as broker, the modern city manager provides one more point of access to the political system for those clamoring to be heard" (p. 43).

Some find the problem-solving-as-politics metaphor objectionable. For example, continuing the "back-to-the-fundamentals" school of city management identified by Stillman (1982), Kirchoff (1990) has written a stinging critique of the facilitation, negotiation, and coordination approach to city management. He criticizes the loss of business management skills among today's local government professionals, asserting: "Way back when, the manager's job was created to apply rational management techniques to the chaos of local government. . . . The only difference now is that we, the so-called professionals, are claiming that governments cannot be operated like businesses" (pp. 2-3). He then identifies two arenas that constitute the universe of local public management—service delivery and community dynamics. Of the latter, he writes: "Politics, power groups, race relations, social issues, and vested interests are among the many variables that constitute this orb. I submit this is primarily the elected officials' sandbox even though we get to play in it more often than we should. We are just the support cast, yet the graduate schools do a better job preparing us for this role than that of our basic task of managing service delivery" (p. 4).

James Griesemer (1990), a former city manager, reinforces this view when he writes: "Political rationality is not the province of managers, but of politicians. The fact that managers must be able to operate in political environments does not mean managers should be politicians" (p. 11).

I suspect that Kirchoff and Griesemer will find many supporters among local government professionals. But implied in their critiques is the assumption that managers choose to act the way they do rather than adapt their behavior to the expectations of others and the context of their work. Their assumption overlooks the possibility that managers have become more political because they have to, not because they want to. Beer, Eisenstat, and Spector (1990) remind us: "Individual behavior is powerfully shaped by the organizational roles that people play. The most effective way to change behavior, therefore, is to put people into a new organizational context, which imposes new roles, responsibilities and relationships on them. This creates a situation that, in a sense, 'forces' new attitudes and behaviors on people" (p. 159). Managers cannot shape the political nature of their environment, but they can and do adapt to it.

Conclusions

I think that managers have become more politically oriented because they need to do their job, not because they are predisposed that way. Having acknowledged a broadening political role, they are now obligated, for their own survival rather than for a traditional professional ideal, to seek political anchors for that role. Acceptance within the community is enhanced as managers speak to fundamental yet abstract values while dealing with specific issues, special interests, and new constituencies. Acceptance is enhanced for the profession as a whole as the values become the basis for professionally sanctioned norms.

Jennings (1987) writes: "In its conception of democracy as being more than majority rule, and in its conception of professionalism as being more than individual conscientious discretion, an ethic of democratic professionalism parts company with both legalism and moralism, but retains the grain of truth each contains. . . . But this ethic of professionalism is primarily a democratic rather than a 'professional' ethic because it situates the professionalism, autonomy, and moral discretion of public administrators within an overarching system of democratic values and processes" (p. 20).

To argue that managers must ground their expanding role in community values is intended as more than a restatement of what I see as an outmoded requirement that the manager do "what is right for the city." Also, it is not meant to imply that managers are unrestricted players in an unbounded political landscape. The distinguishing feature of modern professionalism is the ability to understand and portray with some sophistication the community as a collection of values and to speak to those abstract values through specific issues and interests. In a whipsaw environment where managers risk being seen as no more than politicians, the ability to hold oneself accountable to basic democratic values provides stability and a professional foundation that goes beyond a code of ethics. The next chapter identifies four fundamental values and how contemporary managers engage them.

6

The Value Base of Contemporary Professionalism

Values always have played an important part in defining professionalism in city management. The ICMA adopted its first Code of Ethics in 1924; and we saw in Chapter Five how city managers identify themselves as fulfilling a calling to public service. As local government professionals find themselves involved more in policymaking and community building, the attention and deference they pay to community values increases. As the role expectations of city managers have diversified, so have the values they have responded to in anchoring their professional credibility.

City managers always have characterized themselves as applying rational, analytical approaches in pursuit of the public good. The value "responsiveness" is commonly used to capture the goal of this public service. But the term provides little guidance, as elected and appointed officials justify virtually all decisions in terms of being responsive to the will of the people and to the public good.

Note: Parts of this chapter have appeared in "Tenets of Contemporary Professionalism in Local Government," *Public Administration Review*, 1990, *50*, 654–662.

To restore meaning to the term *responsiveness* in city management, I have divided the concept into four other values: efficiency, representation, social equity, and individual rights. These are fundamental democratic values which, in combination, constitute the conceptual core of public policy debates. When a government is efficient, represents diverse community interests, equitably delivers goods and services, and respects individual rights, it is being responsive.

This chapter examines professionalism in city management in light of these values and suggests that a transformation in professionalism has occurred as efficiency has declined in importance and the other values have ascended.

Tenet III

The value of efficiency still underpins the local government management profession, bringing with it the application of knowledge and expertise to local government problems. But efficiency by itself inadequately describes the value base of professionalism in contemporary city management. Representation, individual rights, and social equity frequently compete with efficiency and have forced upon managers concerns for the authoritative foundations of public policy processes and substance.

Professional Management and Efficiency

Professionalism in local government has hinged durably on administrative expertise and knowledge targeted at building cities and delivering municipal services. Supporting managerial expertise and knowledge is a rational and analytical problem-solving orientation. While efficiency never was solely the criterion of successful decision making for local government professionals, in the orthodox view of public administration it was surely first among contending values.

Earlier, the role of the manager as a broker, negotiator, and consensus builder was identified. But to some, without a predisposition to rational decision making, the manager's contemporary roles would seem hardly distinguishable from the politician's. Bollens and Ries (1969) made this point clearly and without compromise over two decades ago: "It is the extent to which a manager applies expertise and professionalism to the problems of urban government which justifies his position. His political skills make him just like all the other actors on the local government scene. His technical skills make him different. Many factors in the dynamic urban environment force political roles on the manager. Nothing will change this; however, managers have to make a hard choice. Either they must enter the game of politics with gusto and eschew their technical roles, or they must play the much harder role of exploiting their technical skills to influence urban politics. This latter role is demanding indeed, but provides the only justification of city managership as a profession" (p. 48).

This orientation has important roots in the history of city management and in the commonly accepted precept that any professional commands a unique body of specialized knowledge. Even though contemporary political and managerial rhetoric speaks often but vacuously of efficiency, realistically efficiency undergirds the proposition that some solutions to public problems are more rational than others. In short, given a goal, there are some ways to reach that goal that are more direct and less costly and have a better chance of achievement than others.

Norm King (1989), city manager in Palm Springs, California, expresses the efficiency value in what he calls a new approach to public management: "The real meaning of privatization is not the privatization of certain government services by contracting with private enterprises to supply the services, though that may save a little money. The real issue of privatization is to 'privatize' the cost of consuming various resources so that all costs, external and otherwise, are charged to the private user. This and this alone will reduce the *public* costs of having to treat the consequences of over-consumption whether that is too much waste, too little freeway space, or too much air pollution."

While the pressure on some city managers to recognize the rational and analytical base of decision making has not diminished, the source of this pressure in other cases has shifted from managers and the governing body to the increasingly professional administrative staff that works for the manager.

Jack Manahan (1986), director of finance in Johnson County, Kansas, says: "Importance must be continually given to technical competence. City managers must continue to be technically competent so they can continue to make strong recommendations to the council. Managers can't become yes men and just look for the majority. Consensus building is important, but not above everything else. Local government managers have to push their councils to make the right decisons."

In contrast to King and Manahan, Don Blubaugh (1987), city manager in Walnut Creek, California, writes: "A manager today with traditional values may find himself or herself frustrated. Good professional staff work no longer 'cuts it.' I suspect that even being labeled an efficient, professional person will not work to one's best advantage in dealing with the myriad of comments about government being unresponsive, too businesslike, and uncaring of the people it serves" (p. 4).

From the Midwest, Curtis Freeland, city manager in Arkansas City, Kansas, writes: "I think that outright dishonesty and abuse of political power is a long forgotten problem. The legislative reforms on disclosure, open meetings, and public information make a reoccurrence of wholesale abuse unlikely. The old agenda of internal efficiency, professionalism, merit based government is yielding to a new agenda for strong, far reaching initiatives in a battle for a stable and prosperous economy. . . . What we are now seeing is the starting of a trend to swing back towards a larger role for political influence in making decisions at the local level. . . . The public wants movement to enhance and protect the status quo. The political route is perceived as the most effective resource for change" (letter to the author, May 1988).

Former city manager James Griesemer (1990) adds: "Today managers are often required to be more involved with policy than management, more concerned with equity than efficiency, and more sensitive to matters of due process than tangible result. Where once efficiency was valued, now resources are sacrificed on the altar of would-be equity. Where once tangible results counted, now process is product. This is not criticism, it is reality. The realities of the new environment do not fit the traditional technical model of management" (p. 10).

Efficiency is an instrumental value that presupposes agreement on a policy direction. As Thompson (1967) pointed out some years ago, in order to implement the value of efficiency, the internal operations of an organization must be buffered from the threatening uncertainties located in the organization's external environment. Thus, efficiency is useful in only limited contexts for modern city managers who find themselves operating primarily in an external political environment where technical rationality yields to the broader notion of organizational and political rationality.

As Simon ([1945] 1976) predicted, contemporary managers do not appear to maximize rational analytic approaches to decision making, but they do not seek to violate them either. Rationality has become a constraint on public policy-making—it performs the test of sobriety—rather than serving as the driving force (Thomas, 1990).

Among the value trade-offs and compromises the manager frequently makes, the primary ones involve efficiency. A very difficult question for city managers is how far they can compromise the value of efficiency while retaining a solution that will work and which they can accept professionally.

Professional Management and Democracy

As city managers have become politically visible, legitimacy for their role has depended upon anchoring their actions in fundamental values. The idea that public policy-making consists of value trade-offs has focused attention on identifying these competing values and on the role of the manager in incorporating them into public policy-making and administrative processes.

In addition to the value of efficiency, three principles of democratic governance seem to anchor the practice of professional local government management. Redford (1969) identified these as participation, individualism, and equality. Redford's work supports identification here of the crucial values as being *representation, individual rights,* and *social equity,* in addition to *efficiency.* Also supporting this choice is recognition that at least three of these values underpin America's fundamental political institutions. The judicial branch of government protects individual rights largely through due process; legislatures are constituted as representative bodies; and administrative agencies are created to bring knowledge and expertise systematically to bear on public problems.

Representation. In public policy-making bodies, elected officials represent the opinions and demands of citizens, groups of citizens, and special interests. Citizens who will be affected by a public policy should have an opportunity to debate that policy prior to its enactment. In a political process citizen demands and opinions and the power of various advocates are weighed one against another, against the interests of the policymakers themselves, and against precedent to determine which positions should prevail. This initial aspect of representation has to do with the substance of various demands—citizens want something and they want their representatives to carry their demands into the policy-making arena.

Another facet of this value involves the structures that give citizens access to the policy-making process. According to Gottdiener (1987): "Representational forms constitute the opportunity structure for political expression. They can serve directly to constrain political mobilization and canalize it towards specific directions, or, they can also create political resources for groups with links to leadership" (p. 223). In short, some public policy issues will have more to do with how citizen views will be represented than with the substance of those views. We have seen in Chapter Three how the city of Dallas is attempting to deal with its representation problems. Los Angeles County and other local governmental units have been sued under the Voting Rights Act of 1963.

The more heterogeneous a community, the more importance its citizens will place on representation—both on getting their substantive interests realized and finding access for their views. Several managers have noted the downside to this trend. For example, Jan Perkins (1987), deputy city manager in Santa Ana, California, points out: "A group of people may be successful in getting the council to take a particular action which may not be to the benefit of the entire city, but may satisfy the needs of that particular group. . . . A group of twenty-five is a huge outcry, and even then maybe only twenty-five or fifty people may hold that particular point of view, so the rest of the community may not benefit from whatever that particular group is urging" (p. 165).

Tom Downs (1987), former city manager and current secretary of transportation for New Jersey, provides a different view: "The more diverse the councils are, the more I like working in that environment. I like the diversity. I think it is part of the normal, healthy city process. Cities are complex, messy, and conflict oriented. They are melting pots. The more diverse the city council is, the more diverse the politics. They probably better represent the real city. So, it is easier, in some respects, to deal with real problems" (p. 34).

Downs's comments take the profession further away from how the original city managers—drawn largely from the ranks of civil engineers—might think about a problem. Moreover, based on his research in cities in Northern Illinois, Streib (1990) found a direct correlation between the norms of professional management and citizen participation. In other words, city management professionals are more sensitive to representation issues than employees without professional norms.

This sense of professionalism and respect for representation led Sylvester Murray (1987), then city manager of San Diego, to say: "There are some people in the community who appreciate the importance of government and are sophisticated enough to weave it and to mold it so that the quality of their lives is enhanced. There are other people in the community who do not recognize this with the same degree of sophistication. It is the responsibility of managers in government to take the initiative to see that an individual's quality of life is not negatively affected solely because that person does not know how to use the system" (p. 150).

Individual Rights. The value of individual rights connotes legal protection and is expressed, for example, when property owners request rezoning, when public employees invoke merit system or constitutional protection, or when clients of public services seek redress for inequitable treatment. Individual rights frequently are expressed in the due process provisions of administrative decision making.

Individual rights often trump other values because they

claim a legal base in law, including the Constitution. The crux of affirmative action is balancing a public employer's compelling interest in overcoming the effects of discrimination with the individual rights of innocent nonminorities (Nalbandian, 1989). In the case of a public employee's First Amendment right to speak out on public issues, a public employer has the burden of showing that its interests in effective administration outweigh the employee's freedom of expression (*Pickering* v. *Board of Education,* 1968). In the case of drug testing, the government must show that its interests outweigh the individual employee's Fourth Amendment protection from unauthorized search and seizure (*Skinner* v. *Railway Labor Executives' Association,* 1989; *National Treasury Employees Union* v. *William von Raab,* 1989).

Even though individual rights are often dramatically portrayed in the public personnel arena, they command attention in other areas as well. The more powerful the administrative instruments of government become, the more emphasis subjects of that power will place on rights to public notice, hearings, and due process (Rosenbloom, 1987, 1988).

Stewart Margolis (1988), a resident of Inglewood, California, in a letter to the *Los Angeles Times,* expressed the value of individual rights thus: "Rent control is not just impractical or unfairly implemented—it is morally wrong. Property rights are among the most basic rights that all humans have. When the government steps in and tells people what to do with their property (i.e., how much rent they can charge) it violates those rights. It doesn't matter if the majority of voters approve the action. The United States is a constitutional democracy where our freedoms and rights cannot be voted away. That is what distinguishes us from Nazi Germany or the Soviet Union—or at least it used to.''

Social Equity. Social equity as a concept is very similar to the idea of "distributive justice," but with an important difference. Distributive justice is equally relevant in assessing the distribution of public services to individuals or groups. But fairness frequently is calculated in terms of the distribution of goods and services to groups, not individuals (Hero, 1986). The term *social* implies that the unit of analysis is a group or a group characteristic rather than an individual, distinguishing social equity from individual rights. The term *equity* implies some calculation of fairness, right, or justice.

Supreme Court Justice Blackmun implies the term *social equity* in his opinion in *Watson v. Fort Worth Bank and Trust* (1988, p. 2793). In this affirmative action case, he distinguishes between "disparate treatment" where the emphasis is on individual rights, and "disparate impact," where the emphasis is on social equity. Citing *Teamsters* v. *United States,* he writes: "The offense alleged in a disparate-treatment challenge focuses exclusively on the intent of the employer (in disparate-treatment challenge, proof of discriminatory motive is critical). Unless it is proved that an employer intended to disfavor the plaintiff because of his membership in a protected class, a disparate-treatment claim fails. A disparate-impact claim, in contrast, focuses on *effect* of the employment practice (disparate-impact claims involve employment practices that are facially neutral in their treatment of different groups but that in fact fall more harshly on one group than another)" [citations and internal quotation marks omitted].

As another example, the ICMA Declaration of Ideals (International City Management Association, 1982) contains several provisions reflecting social equity:

- Seek balance in the policy formation process through the integration of the social, cultural, and physical aspects of the community.
- Advocate equitable regulation and service delivery, recognizing that needs and expectations for public services may vary throughout the community.
- Take actions to create diverse opportunities in housing, employment, and cultural activity in every community for all people.

The controversial nature of social equity is reflected as it conflicts with the value of efficiency. Joel Valdez (1987), city manager of Tucson, expresses the cost to a local government of pursuing social equity with regard to the homeless: "Another instance of making political decisions involved a shelter for the homeless.

That's a function of existing social service agencies. We're funding them already to the tune of two million dollars a year. There is no reason for the city to be adding another million for soup kitchens. Once you institutionalize something, you can't stop it. For every $30,000 that you allot for the indigent, there is one less cop I can hire" (p. 221).

A study requested by a council member in Dallas showed that just over 80 percent of the unlighted freeways in the city are south of Interstate 30, the poorer and racially diverse part of town. Council member Charles Tandy, who represents part of the area, was quoted as saying, " 'I don't want to believe it's intentional, it's just a mindset that things don't have to be up to the same standard' in southern Dallas" (Jackson, 1990). The newspaper added: "City staff members denied such a mindset and said the state normally initiates freeway lighting. State highway officials said lighting is based largely on traffic volume, which is lower in the south than in the north."

According to scholar (Frederickson, 1980, 1990), politician (Cisneros, 1988), and city manager (Branscome, 1989), social equity is a pivotal American value. Even though America is a society that prizes individualism, one might argue that the moral character and condition of the society is measured by the well-being of its poorest and most underprivileged citizens (Bellah and others, 1985). This belief led Frederickson (1980) to posit "social equity" as the central focus of a new public administration. He added a third pillar to the twin towers of economy and efficiency with the question, "Does this [public] service enhance social equity?" (p. 37). A decade later he suggested, "Efficiency and economy are primarily theories of management while social equity is primarily a theory of government" (1990, p. 229). Branscome (1989) makes a similarly bold statement about city management and social equity: "Equity concerns must be incorporated in today's vision of a community. Heroes foster images, and in the past that image may have been grounded in efficiency. It took heroism to advance efficiency in the midst of corruption, patronage, and favoritism. In the future, we must accept the moral commitment to serve all stakeholders of the community. This requires sensitivity to equity as well as efficiency."

Even though he endorses the value of social equity, like Valdez, Branscome cannot escape the tension between social equity and efficiency. He tempers his own advocacy by saying, "Cost effectiveness is the defining characteristic of city management, and social equity cannot be pursued in the absence of it."

While social equity plays a consciousness-raising and educative role in our communities, paradoxically it does so without an institutional advocate. Legislatures are responsible for the value of representation; individual rights falls under the courts' jurisdiction; and efficiency has its home in public bureaucracies. In short, there is no institution of government that has as its central presupposition the fostering of social equity; there is no institutional advocate. Thus, social equity is a value that is easier to endorse politically than to realize in city hall. It is a concern more likely to be raised through timely public debate and legislation than routinized in administrative process or governing institutions.

Sylvester Murray hints at the special and vulnerable nature of social equity: "I have specifically not referred to these racial and ethnic groups as 'special interest groups' because they are not of the same mold as those who are trying to get a direct financial or special favor in the 'good old boy' sense. Whereas the special interest group usually invests money (political contributions) for a quid pro quo effect, the racial or ethnic group does not" (letter to the author, July 1989).

Reflecting on the social equity orientation in the International City Management Association's Declaration of Ideals, ICMA executive director, William Hansell (1990), commented that the declaration has not been incorporated into the profession of city management on a par with the Code of Ethics.

Implications of a Values Perspective

Value Trade-offs and Responsiveness. The concept of responsiveness has always held a central place in the professional practice of city management. From a values perspective, responsiveness is measured by the weights attached to the different values. For example, in a simple case, if an elected official's constituents place a higher priority on social equity than efficiency, the constituents are likely to view as responsive the elected official who shares their priorities. In this sense, one might then argue that a value profile might be drawn for a community, or perhaps more realistically for segments of a community. The difficulty, of course, is eliciting or inferring the profile (Hall-Saltzstein, 1985). The benefit of the values perspective is that it helps conceptualize the political community and the conflicts that frequently characterize public policy development. Thus, by framing policy issues in terms of specific values, it has the potential to help a community and its officials discuss public purposes.

The following case illustrates the utility of the values framework in conceptualizing a public policy conflict. To develop the case as a learning tool, I have embellished the basic situation that arose in Lawrence, Kansas, in the late 1980s.

> Lawrence is a university community of about 60,000 permanent residents. Its economy grows steadily, and good government is the norm.
>
> Lawrence has been growing toward the western edge of town where new homes are built at a cost substantially higher than the median cost of homes in the city. Construction of the new homes and supporting retail development require a lot of concrete, and the owner of one of the largest concrete suppliers operates from the southeastern edge of the city where there is little residential development.
>
> The owner of the concrete plant (who would become a city commissioner at the next election) requested that property he owned in western Lawrence be rezoned so he could build a concrete supply facility nearer to the work he was performing.
>
> The request immediately stirred controversy because homeowners in this upper- and upper-middle-class area said the facility would cause powdery dust and heavy truck traffic. Their letters to the editor and contacts with city commissioners conveyed their concern that their interests be adequately understood and represented. [Value of representation.]

The owner replied that he owned the property! He ought to be able to decide on its use as long as his proposal was reasonable. [Value of individual rights.] He said, "What good does it do to own a piece of property if I cannot use it the way I intend? My proposal does not hurt anyone, and it is clearly an appropriate use for the land."

The planning commission requested a recommendation from the planning staff. [Value of efficiency.] Staff concluded that there were no planning principles or regulations that would prohibit the rezoning request. Neighbors in the affected area, which included many long-time owners of businesses in Lawrence and a new group of business executives, renewed their vociferous objections. [Value of representation.]

The homeowners carried their case to the publisher of the local newspaper who wrote an editorial recommending denial of the rezoning request, suggesting that common sense [representation] prevail over "blind professionalism" [efficiency] and individual interests [individual rights]. The city commission expected a full house if the planning commission granted the rezoning request.

In the meantime, the residents of east Lawrence, a lower socioeconomic and racially diverse neighborhood, began to grumble. They sensed the tide turning in favor of the west Lawrence residents. According to the newspaper, east Lawrence neighborhood spokespersons were charging that if the property were on the east side of town in their neighborhood, there would not be such a fuss, and the property would be rezoned. [Value of social equity.]

The brevity of this case conceals its complexity. In a value sense, this public policy issue is very complicated and will test the political skills of the elected commission and the city manager. With this case, the city commissioners will express their value preferences, reflecting their sense of public priorities, and they are sure to displease someone. Depending on the commission's decision, some citizens will consider them responsive and others unresponsive. (It was resolved with the city manager taking the initiative and successfully persuading the property owner to withdraw his rezoning request.)

Having related this case, I want to make three points about the values perspective it implies. First, communities and segments of communities can be characterized and differentiated by their value profile. Clearly, some segments in Dallas, for example, are more interested in a rational, analytical approach to government as a business, as distinguished from other parts that place more emphasis on representation and social equity, focusing often on the implications that "rational" decisions have on the distribution of public services.

Second, as public policy-making has become so complex and potentially conflictual, managers can help clarify and organize policy discussions if they are able to express the values contained in the different viewpoints and in the consequences of various decisions. By doing this, they can help their governing bodies develop coherence in public policy-making. Individual issues that seem unconnected may contain a value theme for those prepared to view policy-making in terms of values.

Third, to repeat the words of Charles Anderson (1986), former city manager in Dallas, "It takes a lot of vigilance and a lot of energy to stay neutral but influential." Diversity has a way of dominating debate and psychologically consuming the participants. Thus, even though value conflicts can help a community learn about itself, they have the potential to be destructive. In a similar vein, Bellah (1985) has observed, "For all the lip service given to respect for cultural differences, Americans seem to lack the resources to think about the relationships between groups that are culturally, socially, and economically quite different" (p. 206).

The negotiating, brokering, and coordinating skills prized by contemporary managers result from the need to deal with differences in a community. They suggest that part of the answer to dealing with differences focuses the manager's attention on governing "processes" as well as on the substance of public policy.

Public Policy Processes and Substance. City management has become as concerned with the creation and nurturing of governmental processes in a community as with the efficient and effective delivery of municipal services (Stillman, 1982; Kirchoff, 1990). The activities—whether political or administrative—that are continually required to nurture a civic culture are nested in the values that are sought. In other words, the process of searching for what a community values, its direction and sense of purpose, must incorporate the values that the inquiry seeks. It is essential to recognize the values of representation, individual rights, and social equity, as well as efficiency, because governing processes, whether political or administrative, gain credibility when they reflect sustaining values that underpin a community's political culture.

The danger in accentuating process is the tendency to become satisfied with compromise or consensus which provides no long-term direction. The goal of the facilitator is to secure an agreement; there is no winning and losing, and there are no right or wrong agreements. In this vein Bellah (1985) notes: "We're getting so good at process, it deflects from substance. This is why values bring us back to substance and to ethics" (p. 21).

One is left with the ambiguous guidance that substance and process are both important to local government professionals. Kirchoff's paper (1990) calling for more attention to the basics of service delivery adds to Stillman's earlier discovery (1982) of a "back-to-the-basics" school of city management and suggests that the substance/process debate is not dead. What differentiates today's managers from their predecessors is, first, the emphasis noted in Chapter Four on "democratizing" administrative processes as well as policy-making activities, and second, the idea that values in general provide substance. It is not only the professional's judgment that is substantive. For example, hammering out a political consensus revealing the ascendant value of individual rights signals political priorities, provides broad substantive direction, and permits administrative systems to adjust and to reflect the value.

The City Manager As Educator. The manager is ethically obligated to participate in an educational process that contributes to a shared understanding of the multiple value perspectives brought to public policy questions. The four values that underpin contemporary professionalism frequently define one another. Social equity in an affirmative action debate is given meaning when contrasted with the individual rights of nonminorities. Rational analytic thinking reflecting the value of efficiency is given shape when contrasted with representational interests. Thus, in Kaufman's historical view (1956) of government reform, "The defense of any one [value] was often framed in terms of advancement of the others simultaneously. The story is thus one of changing balance among the values, not of total displacement" (p. 1067). Friedrich (1963) adds, "Justice and injustice cannot be related to any *one* value, be it equality or any other, but only to the complex value system of a man, a community, or mankind" (p. 199).

Policy-making is a process where contexts are created, where people can critically evaluate and revise what they believe (Reich, 1988a). The broader the context and the range of values entertained, the more encompassing the potential community one can forge and the more realistically a community can design its future. A value system oriented around simple conflicts between representational interests in the governing body and efficiency—a rational, analytic staff perspective—limits a manager in today's heterogeneous political environments where the simplest of policy issues masks complex value positions.

City managers have accepted a role as educator, and this helps them fulfill the ethical goal of stimulating debate about political values. It would seem reasonable to assign to elected officials the educative role we have been outlining. But in some ways, city managers are better prepared to act as educators. Council members are elected to *allocate* values and make public policy decisions; city managers educate citizens and council members about the values from which public policies emerge.

Managers (Bonsey, 1987; Gaebler, 1987; and Tipton, 1989) as well as academicians (Hale, 1989; Svara, 1989a) acknowledge this role. Howard Tipton (1989), city manager in Daytona Beach, observes: "The manager is in the center of information flow from city staff, city council and citizens. The use of knowledge to educate the community is a primary responsibility of the manager" (p. 178).

Usually, managers express their educational role in terms of selling a particular policy. For example, Osmond Bonsey (1987), town manager in Yarmouth, Maine, and past president of the International City Management Association, second-guessed his own effectiveness, commenting, "Our mistake, my mistake, was in not providing the education and leadership needed to make sure the zoning program passed" (p. 9).

Svara's work (1989a) defines the role more broadly and more in keeping with the ethical purposes of stimulating political debate: "The manager should develop direct ties with a wide range of groups and organizations in the community for several reasons. One, the manager is seen as a major participant in the political process and cannot remain aloof. Two, the manager and staff are primary sources of information for the public about much of what city government does. Three, the manager will need to be able to directly communicate his or her perspective on issues to the public at large and to friendly audiences as the council is less able and inclined to do so" (pp. 203–204).

While city managers would seem to occupy an ideal position to carry out an educative role, according to James Blagg (1987), city manager in Abilene, Texas, "interpreting community values is a new role for managers." He points to the emerging use of citizen surveys, newspaper polls, and focus groups of citizens as ways of gathering information. However, the means of gathering information about public wants far exceeds a government's capacity to discern the values behind those wants and to transform them into public policy.

Perhaps the biggest obstacle to having managers fill an educative role is their predisposition as problem solvers. Those who solve problems seek convergence not divergence of opinion. As Simon ([1945] 1976) pointed out some time ago, managerial problem solving is designed with a "satisficing" criterion in mind; managers will sacrifice an optimal solution for a satisfactory one that will work in order to move on to other business. It is the premature transformation of a policy debate into a problem-to-be-solved which frequently leads to charges of administrative unresponsiveness. Reich (1988b) points out that social learning, a community learning about its own values, is an elusive undertaking that contrasts with effective decision making and successful implementation.

Not all issues provoke self-examination; reflection costs time, and with political discourse often comes the babble of ideologues, the shrill sounds of demagogues, and the droning on of those who cannot see beyond the first tree on the median. Most sobering of all is Reich's reminder (1988b, p. 146) that deliberation does not automatically generate reasoned public ideas; it merely creates the preconditions for them to arise.

Conclusions

In an increasingly complex political climate characterized by political fragmentation, special interests, and personal ambition, a values perspective provides the manager with stability. Values transcend particular issues and interests, and I believe that the four identified in this chapter—efficiency, representation, individual rights, and social equity—are fundamental and durable politically.

Political responsiveness has become a nebulous term, often used to justify whatever decision has been made. A values perspective grounds the concept and can further debate about public policy. Potentially, it provides the themes and basic elements of a framework necessary to build political and administrative coherence and direction.

The ability to identify, understand, and engage these diverse and often conflicting values has become essential to effective professionalism. As managers are involved more in policy-making and community building, they provide political interests access to governing processes and power. Advocates of these interests are not satisfied to have managers fall back on their subordinate role to the governing body to justify their role and actions. It seems to me that in this environment, where political accountability is going to become more important, it will become impossible for managers to be value neutral or above politics. The most they can hope for is to avoid capture by any one value interest and to seek consciously to balance value diversity in their thinking and actions.

7

The Future of Professionalism
in Local Government

The history of professionalism in local government has seen the city manager's role evolve with visible policy-making aspects involving the negotiation and brokerage of community power. This role differs considerably from the value-neutral, administrative expert envisioned by the orthodox perspective of council-manager government. Recent history has seen significant efforts to legitimize the manager's discernible political power. Managers have succeeded in grounding in a broad base of community values their own position and the administrative processes they oversee. They are gradually accepting the challenge that values like representation, individual rights, and social equity pose for efficiency, the traditional cornerstone of professionalism in city management.

We have discussed in this book three transformations from the orthodox view of city management. City management has moved from a politics/administration dichotomy to the sharing of governmental functions between elected and appointed officials; from political neutrality and formal accountability to political sensitivity and responsiveness to community values themselves; from efficiency as the core value to efficiency, representation, individual rights, and social equity as a complex array of values anchoring professionalism.

Perhaps underlying these transformations is the local government professional's growing acceptance that the city is a political and social as well as an economic unit and that managers cannot deal with the one without attending to the other. As important as jobs and a growing tax base are for a city, its viability depends as well on its capacity to make collective decisions in a context of growing diversity and interests. In this vein, the tolerance, respect, and truthfulness that characterize relationships among citizens are precious virtues. Government nurtures these virtues as it encourages reflective citizenship—a thoughtful understanding of the citizens' expectations of and obligations to the community. It is commonly understood that reflective citizenship cannot be taught; it must be learned by doing. Thus, the process of governance is often government's most important product. If the decision-making process which leads to what is "right" for the city alienates the investment in the community of a significant minority, it may not be the "right" course of action, after all.

"Taking action when everyone wants to be involved in the act," a theme of the ICMA's Future Visions task force, poses a formidable challenge for both appointed and elected officials. Elected officials and local government professionals at all levels will find themselves increasingly frustrated if they lack consensus-building skills and a tolerance for solutions that will work, as opposed to the "best" solutions.

Greater appreciation of the expanded value base of successful city management represents a trend which grows out of the appreciation that professionalism in local government has changed significantly over the years. But a city management profession grounded firmly in a set of identifiable values reinforces the history of city management. It is clear that the simple value pair of responsiveness and efficiency has given way to a more complex array of values, but the notion that professionalism is grounded in values is not foreign to professionalism in local government.

In a turbulent environment, values represent anchors; they stabilize analyses and join what might otherwise seem to be disjointed events and forces (Emery and Trist, 1975; Schon, 1973). Thus, it seems likely that the search for an empirically sound value base that also places the practice of city management within a democratic context will continue as long as managers work in unstable, heterogeneous environments.

In environments of political, economic, and social turbulence, those managers who continue to tie their professionalism to the structure of council-manager government probably will be disappointed. To this day, there are managers who believe that the decision in 1969 to admit non-city managers into membership in the ICMA was a mistake that diluted the standards and ethos of the profession. But the structural trends are clear. Cities are not giving up on council-manager government, but they are asking it to adapt, to serve the political needs that are perceived in individual cities.

It is becoming increasingly difficult to differentiate council-manager from strong-mayor cities because the pure types of either are disappearing. Even ICMA data analyses are confounded by the predominance of hybrid governmental forms (Renner, 1988).

Structural reforms are the product of political campaigns, and the results speak to political compromise, not structural integrity. But while pure types of governmental structures disappear, the need for professionalism in local government will not; this is clear. Charter reforms do seem to call for more representation and political leadership, but curiously they do so in most cases without wanting to sacrifice professionalism. More representation and more equity without sacrificing rational-analytical thinking seems to be a trend in governmental reform. The reason is simple. In complex urban environments, public policy cannot be formulated without technical and specialized knowledge and information. Thus, while some may see a trend away from pure council-manager government, paradoxically perhaps, there is a trend toward more professional managers in local governments regardless of governmental form.

In short, it is the values and the practices of managers that increasingly will define professionalism in local government, not where city managers work or who hires or fires them. Successful professional managers are and will continue to be those who are able to identify, understand, and work with the values of their community. In part, they will connect to their governing body through these values—it will provide an understanding upon which they can communicate—even if they can only sense the values and not articulate them. But more important, grounding the profession in enduring values like efficiency, representation, individual rights, and social equity extends professional obligations beyond responsibility solely to the elected representatives and to the citizens themselves.

With this broad set of obligations and without the politics/administration dichotomy as a shield, the manager becomes a political actor and a moral agent. But the craft of local government professionalism will hinge in part on the manager's ability to make political decisions as well as moral and other value judgments without appearing to be a politician.

This sounds manipulative, and to some it will appear unseemly; I do not mean it to be. The world of any organization is phenomenological. It is more the product of social constructions and tacit agreement among the participants than most of us choose to recognize. Thus, managers are able to proclaim honestly and with conviction that "policy-making is problem solving and not politics" if their communications with others reinforces that view.

I am convinced that councils and managers define and then make judgments about "political" behavior differently from city to city and from context to context. While identification of "political behavior" may be easy for outside observers who set out to measure it objectively with predetermined and standard criteria, I suspect for the participants of governance it is not that simple. The same manager acting the same way but working for two different councils, or even the same council but at different times, may be perceived in one instance as acting politically and in another as acting administratively.

It seems to me that the key to this perception rests largely in the motives of the manager. As McClelland (1976) discovered, executives share a strong drive for power. But for the successful ones, that power is perceived to be targeted toward the greater good as opposed to personal gain. Thus, subordinates are inclined to ally themselves with some executives and protect themselves from others.

Therefore, one might argue as a basic proposition that a manager acting politically but virtuously walks on firm ground. MacIntyre (1984) works through a complex philosophical analysis to reach the point of identifying as virtues justice, courage, and honesty. He suggests that virtues are exhibited in practices where

"goods internal to that form of activity are realized in the course of
trying to achieve . . . standards of excellence . . . appropriate to . . .
that . . . activity" (p. 187). Liberally interpreting MacIntyre, one
might suggest that the virtues of justice, courage, and honesty are
essential to the practice of city management, *and* they are the result
of that practice.

In terms of the "political" city manager, I would suggest that
managers who seek to advance the public good through virtuous
practice are likely to rise to the top of their profession. John Dever
(1987), city manager in Long Beach, California, eloquently com-
bines the notion of virtue and power in this statement: "A major
project in a city today takes 7-12 years to plan, finance, and realize.
How do you get people who are only interested in the next election
or how good they look today to participate in this process? It takes
council courage and managerial courage—sacrifice—and some
communities demand it. Some cities get it through leadership by the
council, mayor, or manager—or a combination. The manager must
provide whatever assistance is needed, if there is political leadership. If there is none, the manager must foster it—sometimes by
taking the lead" (p. 19).

If managers ground their virtuous practice in enduring political values, the politics/administration dichotomy would appear
obsolete. But I do not think this is possible. There is a fundamental
philosophical discussion that the dichotomy stimulates. As we have
seen, a crucial question for observers of the administrative state is
how to bring expert and specialized knowledge to bear on public
policy-making while retaining the supremacy of political values.
Posing the dichotomy encourages discussions of this question by
examining the boundaries of politics and administration, even
though the boundaries are impossible to define (March and Olsen,
1989). The dichotomy is less important as an answer to the question
than as a stimulus to its consideration.

One might suggest that council-manager government simply
provides the most convenient venue for this important discussion.
The council-manager plan captures two of the essential assumptions of contemporary political life: organizations are rational, and
politics are value laden. Few other institutional settings operate as

clearly on these assumptions; therefore, the discussion is more focused in council-manager government.

The city manager is a prototypical character in our society. He or she operates at the interstices of political and administrative constellations of logic. On the one hand, the manager understands that politics is a game played by representatives of interests who use power to resolve value conflicts. On the other hand, the manager comprehends administration as problem solving among a community of experts who exchange information in a spirit of harmony and cooperation. Understanding the logic of administrative thinking, the manager acts as an intermediary to elected officials. And, privy to communication with and between elected officials, the manager translates political logic into administrative goals and objectives. Thus, as long as the question of political supremacy over administration is salient, we will be concerned with the roles, responsibilities, and values of the city management profession, even as the pure council-manager plan yields to more hybrid forms.

I believe that the practice of local government professionals is an essential part of our learning about democracy because public administration scholars cannot avoid the question of how governments can bring knowledge to bear on public policy-making while retaining the supremacy of political values. The blurry line between what is political and what is administrative will continue to disintegrate because political values provide the essential legitimacy for administrative practice; and administrative experts provide essential information for informed public policy-making. But the theoretical question will remain, and the test of the answer will be its ability to describe what local government professionals do day to day and its facility in placing their practice within the context of a democratic theory.

With the three tenets proposed in this book, I have tried to codify city management practice. The tenets are not new because the practices they describe are not new. They are newly formulated, and against them city managers now can set their craft and continue the crucial dialogue about the roles, responsibilities, and values of local government professionals.

References

"A Better City Budget Next Time." *Kansas City Times,* Apr. 24, 1989, p. A-6.

Aberbach, J. D., Putnam, R. D., and Rockman, B. A. *Bureaucrats and Politicians in Western Democracies.* Cambridge, Mass.: Harvard University Press, 1981.

Abney, G., and Lauth, T. P. "Influence of the Chief Executive on City Line Agencies." *Public Administration Review,* 1982, *42* (Mar.-Apr.), 135-143.

Abney, G., and Lauth, T. P. *The Politics of State and City Administration.* Albany, State University of New York Press, 1986.

Ackoff, R. L. "The Future of Operational Research." *Journal of the Operational Research Society,* 1979, *30* (2), 93-104.

Adrian, C. R. "Forms of City Government in American History." *Municipal Yearbook.* Washington, D.C.: International City Management Association, 1988.

Ammons, D. N., and Newell, C. " 'City Managers Don't Make Policy': A Lie; Let's Face It." *National Civic Review,* 1988, *57,* 124-132.

Anderson, C. Interviewed by Arthur Davis. Lawrence: Department of Public Administration, University of Kansas, Apr. 20, 1986.

Anderson, E. A. "Response to 'City Management at a Crossroads.' " In H. G. Frederickson (ed.), *Ideal and Practice in Council-Manager Government.* Washington, D.C.: International City Management Association, 1989.

Appleby, P. *Policy and Administration.* University: University of Alabama Press, 1949.

Banfield, E. C., and Wilson, J. Q. *City Politics.* New York: Vintage Books, 1966.

Banovetz, J. M. (ed.). *Managing the Modern City.* Washington, D.C.: International City Management Association, 1971.

Barrett, R. A., and Harmon, B. D. *External Relationships of City Councils.* Urban Data Service, *4* (3). Washington, D.C.: International City Management Association, 1972.

Barta, C. "Dallas Needs a Change." *Dallas Morning News,* Jan. 30, 1989, p. 11A.

Beer, M., Eisenstat, R. A., and Spector, B. "Why Change Programs Don't Produce Change." *Harvard Business Review,* 1990, *68* (Nov.-Dec.), 146-158.

Bellah, R. N., and others. *Habits of the Heart: Individualism and Commitment in American Life.* Berkeley: University of California Press, 1985.

Blagg, J. Comments to the Texas Municipal League, Fort Worth, Texas, Oct. 8, 1987.

Blubaugh, D. A. "The Changing Role of the Public Administrator." *Public Management,* 1987, *69* (June), 7-10.

Bollens, J. C., and Ries, J. C. *The City Manager Profession: Myths and Realities.* Chicago: Public Administration Service, 1969.

Bonsey, O. Interviewed in J. Nalbandian and R. G. Davis (eds.), *Reflections of Local Government Professionals.* Lawrence: Department of Public Administration, University of Kansas, 1987.

Booth, D. A. "Are Elected Mayors a Threat to Managers?" *Administrative Science Quarterly,* 1968, *12* (Mar.), 572-589.

Bosworth, K. A. "The Manager *Is* a Politician." *Public Administration Review,* 1958, *18* (Summer), 216-222.

Boynton, R. P., and Wright, D. S. "Mayor-Manager Relationships in Large Council-Manager Cities: A Reinterpretation." *Public Administration Review,* 1971, *31,* 28-36.

Branscome, C. "The Need for Heroes in City Management." Presentation to the annual meeting of City Managers, University of Kansas, Lawrence, Apr. 26, 1989.

Bromage, A. W. *Urban Policy Making: The Council Manager Partnership.* Chicago: Public Administration Service, 1964.

Brown, L. J. "Response to 'Policy and Administration: City Managers As Comprehensive Professional Leaders.'" In H. G. Frederickson (ed.), *Ideal and Practice in Council-Manager Government*. Washington, D.C.: International City Management Association, 1989.

Burns, J. M. *Leadership*. New York: Harper & Row, 1978.

Cabanatuan, M. "Hercules a Bit Different, Even in Ballot Measures." *West County Times*, Mar. 6, 1988, pp. 1, 2A.

Carman, B. "Gresham Considers Making Mayor a Paid, Full-Time Job." *Oregonian*, Feb. 25, 1988.

Childs, R. S. "The Theory of the New Controlled Executive Plan." *National Municipal Review*, 1913, 2 (Jan.). Reprinted in E. C. Mabie (ed.), *City Manager Plan of Government*. New York: H. W. Wilson, 1918.

Childs, R. S. *First 50 Years of the Council-Manager Plan of Municipal Government*. New York: National Municipal League, 1965.

Childs, R. S., Waite, H. M., and others. "Professional Standards and Professional Ethics in the New Profession of City Manager." *National Municipal Review*, 1916, 5 (Apr.). Reprinted in E. C. Mabie (ed.), *City Manager Plan of Government*. New York: H. W. Wilson, 1918.

Cisneros, H. Presentation to the annual meeting of the International City Management Association, Charlotte, N.C., Oct. 26, 1988.

City Managers' Association. *Proceedings of the First Annual Convention of The City Managers' Association*. Springfield, Ohio: City Managers' Association, 1914.

City Managers' Association. *Proceedings of the Third Annual Meeting*. St. Augustine, Fla.: City Managers' Association, 1916.

Coile, N. "The City Manager Who Never Takes No for an Answer." *Governing*, 1988, 1 (Oct.), 45–49.

Cooper, T. L. *An Ethic of Citizenship for Public Administration*. Englewood Cliffs, N.J.: Prentice-Hall, 1991.

"Council vs. Bureaucrats." Kansas City *Times*, Aug., 23, 1988, p. A-6.

Crane, R. T. *Digest of City Manager Charters*. New York: National Municipal League, 1923.

Crawford, S., and Housewright, E. "Charter Review Panel Abruptly Stops Work." *Dallas Morning News*, May 30, 1989, pp. 1A, 11A.

Dever, J. Interviewed in J. Nalbandian and R. G. Davis (eds.), *Re-*

flections of Local Government Professionals. Lawrence: Department of Public Administration, University of Kansas, 1987.

"Directly Elected Mayor Instills Leadership, Continuity." *Fort Collins Coloradoan,* May 14, 1989, p. B7.

Downs, T. Interviewed in J. Nalbandian and R. G. Davis (eds.), *Reflections of Local Government Professionals.* Lawrence: Department of Public Administration, University of Kansas, 1987.

Edwards, J. T., Nalbandian, J., and Wedel, K. "Individual Values and Professional Education: Implications for Practice and Education." *Administration and Society,* 1981, *13,* 123–143.

Ehrenhalt, A. "How a Liberal Government Came to Power in a Conservative Suburb." *Governing,* 1988, *1* (Mar.), 51–56.

Ehrenhalt, A. "The New City Manager Is." *Governing,* 1990, *3,* (Sept.), 40–46.

Emery, F. E., and Trist, E. L. *Towards a Social Ecology.* New York: Plenum, 1975.

"End Charade; Elect Mayor." *Fort Collins Coloradoan,* May 14, 1989, p. B6.

Fitzpatrick, J. C. "Plan Would Let Council Choose Bond Advisers." *Kansas City Times,* Dec. 17, 1988, pp. A-1, A-21.

Fitzpatrick, J. C. "Council Coalition Leaving Its Mark on Budget." *Kansas City Times,* Apr. 30, 1989, pp. A-1, A-11.

Flournoy, C. "Housing Inquiry Promised." Dallas *Morning News,* May 2, 1989, pp. 1A, 5A.

Flournoy, C. "Council Bypassed on Housing Rehab, Rucker Says." Dallas *Morning News,* May 18, 1989, pp. 33–34A.

Foell, D. Interviewed in J. Nalbandian and R. G. Davis (eds.), *Reflections of Local Government Professionals.* Lawrence: Department of Public Administration, University of Kansas, 1987.

"For Strong Mayor System." *Toledo Blade,* Nov. 4, 1989, p. 6.

Frederickson, H. G. *The New Public Administration.* University: University of Alabama Press, 1980.

Frederickson, H. G. "Public Administration and Social Equity." *Public Administration Review,* 1990, *50,* 228–237.

Friedrich, C. J. *The Philosophy of Law in Historical Perspective.* (2nd ed.) Chicago: University of Chicago Press, 1963.

Gaebler, T. Interviewed in J. Nalbandian and R. G. Davis (eds.),

Reflections of Local Government Professionals. Lawrence: Department of Public Administration, University of Kansas, 1987.

Goodnow, F. J. *Politics and Administration: A Study in Government.* New York: Russell and Russell, 1900, reissued 1967.

Gottdiener, M. *The Decline of Urban Politics.* Newbury Park, Calif.: Sage Publications, 1987.

Green, R. E. *Local Government Managers: Styles and Challenges.* Baseline Data Report, *19* (2). Washington, D.C.: International City Management Association, 1987.

Griesemer, J. R. "Restoring Relevance to Local Government Management." *Public Management,* 1990, *72* (Sept.), 7–12.

Gruber, J. E. *Controlling Bureaucracies: Dilemmas in Governance.* Berkeley: University of California Press, 1987.

Gulick, L. "Science, Values and Public Administration." In L. Gulick and L. Urwick (eds.), *Papers on the Science of Administration.* New York: Institute of Public Administration, 1937.

Gulick, L., and Urwick, L. (eds.). *Papers on the Science of Administration.* New York: Institute of Public Administration, 1937.

Haber, S. *Efficiency and Uplift: Scientific Management in the Progressive Era 1890–1920.* Chicago: University of Chicago Press, 1964.

Hale, M. L. "The Nature of City Managers' Work." In H. G. Frederickson (ed.), *Ideal and Practice in Council-Manager Government.* Washington, D.C.: International City Management Association, 1989.

Hall-Saltzstein, G. "Conceptualizing Bureaucratic Responsiveness." *Administration and Society,* 1985, *17* (3), 283–306.

Hansell, W. Interviewed by John Nalbandian, Lawrence, Kans., Apr. 23, 1990.

Hays, S. P. "The Politics of Reform in Municipal Government in the Progressive Era." *Pacific Northwest Quarterly,* 1964, *55,* 157–189.

Herchert, R. Interviewed by Ardenia Holland. Lawrence: Department of Public Administration, University of Kansas, Apr. 20, 1986.

Hero, R. E. "The Urban Service Delivery Literature: Some Questions and Considerations." *Polity,* 1986, *18,* 659–677.

Hickey, N. Interviewed in J. Nalbandian and R. G. Davis (eds.),

Reflections of Local Government Professionals. Lawrence: Department of Public Administration, University of Kansas, 1987.

Hinton, D. W., and Kerrigan, J. E. "Tracing the Changing Knowledge and Skill Needs and Service Activities of Public Managers." In H. G. Frederickson (ed.), *Ideal and Practice in Council-Manager Government.* Washington, D.C.: International City Management Association, 1989.

Hofstadter, R. *The Age of Reform.* New York: Vintage Books, 1955.

Housewright, E. "Ragsdale, Lipscomb Seek Vote on Charter." *Dallas Morning News,* Feb. 26, 1989, pp. 21A, 23A.

Housewright, E., and Weiss, J. "Council Is Wary of Report." *Dallas Morning News,* Jan. 14, 1989, pp. 1A, 5A.

Huntley, R. J., and Macdonald, R. J. "Urban Managers: Organizational Preferences, Managerial Styles, and Social Policy Roles." *Municipal Yearbook.* Washington, D.C.: International City Management Association, 1975.

International City Management Association. *ICMA Declaration of Ideals.* Washington, D.C.: International City Management Association, 1982.

International City Management Association. "ICMA Code of Ethics with Guidelines." *Public Management,* 1984, *66* (Feb.), 10.

International City Management Association. 1988 State of the Profession Survey Results. *ICMA Newsletter,* Nov. 21, 1988. Washington, D.C.: International City Management Association.

Jackson, D. "Unlighted Freeways in Southern Dallas Decried." *Dallas Morning News,* June 14, 1990, p. 29A.

Jennings, B. "Public Administration: In Search of Democratic Professionalism." *The Hastings Center Report,* 1987, *17* (Feb.), 18–20.

Kammerer, G. "Role Diversity of City Managers." *Administrative Science Quarterly,* 1964, *8* (Mar.), 421–442.

Katz, D., and Kahn, R. L. *The Social Psychology of Organizing.* (2nd ed.) New York: Wiley, 1978.

Kaufman, H. "Emerging Conflicts in the Doctrines of Public Administration." *American Political Science Review,* 1956, *50* (4), 1057–1073.

Keane, M. Interviewed in J. Nalbandian and R. G. Davis (eds.),

Reflections of Local Government Professionals. Lawrence: Department of Public Administration, University of Kansas, 1987.

Kelley, C. "Lesser Says He'll Seek Mayor's Post." *Dallas Morning News,* Feb. 2, 1989, pp. 1A, 10A.

Kelley, C. "Most in Poll Back Altering City Charter." *Dallas Morning News,* Feb. 20, 1989, pp. 1A, 7A.

King, N. R. "Managing the Demand for Government Services: New Directions for City Management." Presented at the 42nd annual meeting of City Managers, University of Kansas, Lawrence, Apr. 26, 1989.

Kipp, R. Interviewed in J. Nalbandian and R. G. Davis (eds.), *Reflections of Local Government Professionals.* Lawrence: Department of Public Administration, University of Kansas, 1987.

Kirchoff, W. "Babbit Could Have Been a City Manager." *Public Management,* 1990, 72 (Sept.), 2-6.

Krislov, S., and Rosenbloom, D. H. *Representative Bureaucracy and the American Political System.* New York: Praeger, 1981.

Lane, L. M., and Wolf, J. F. *The Human Resource Crisis in the Public Sector.* New York: Quorum Books, 1990.

Lipset, S. M. *Political Man: The Social Basis of Politics.* In W. Connolly (ed.), *Legitimacy and the State.* New York: New York University Press, 1984.

Lowi, T. J. *The End of Liberalism.* (2nd ed.) New York: Norton, 1979.

Lukas, A. J. "Needed in Yonkers: Old Fashioned Politics." *Public Management,* 1988, 70 (Dec.), 2-3.

McClelland, D. "Power Is the Great Motivator." *Harvard Business Review,* 1976, 54 (Mar.-Apr.), 100-110.

MacIntyre, A. *Beyond Virtue.* Notre Dame, Ind.: University of Notre Dame, 1984.

Managing for Social and Economic Opportunity. Washington, D.C.: International City Management Association, 1969.

Manahan, J. Interviewed by Steven D. Powers. Lawrence: Department of Public Administration, University of Kansas, Apr. 20, 1986.

March, J. G., and Olsen, J. *Rediscovering Institutions.* New York: Free Press, 1989.

Margolis, S. Letter to the Editor. *Los Angeles Times*, Aug. 8, 1988, p. II-4.

Minkin, P. "Salary Support." *Lawrence Journal World*, May 17, 1989.

Mooney, J. D. "The Principles of Organization." In L. Gulick and L. Urwick (eds.), *Papers on the Science of Administration*. New York: Institute of Public Administration, 1937.

Mora, D. Interviewed in J. Nalbandian and R. G. Davis (eds.), *Reflections of Local Government Professionals*. Lawrence: Department of Public Administration, University of Kansas, 1987.

Mosher, F. C. *Democracy and the Public Service*. (2nd ed.) New York: Oxford University Press, 1982.

Mulrooney, K. F. "Prologue: Can City Managers Deal Effectively with Major Social Problems?" *Public Administration Review*, 1971, *31* (Jan.-Feb.), 6-14.

Murray, S. Interviewed in J. Nalbandian and R. G. Davis (eds.), *Reflections of Local Government Professionals*. Lawrence: Department of Public Administration, University of Kansas, 1987.

Nalbandian, J. "The Supreme Court's 'Consensus' on Affirmative Action." *Public Administration Review*, 1989, *49* (Jan.-Feb.), 38-45.

Nalbandian, J., and Davis, R. G. (eds.). *Reflections of Local Government Professionals*. Lawrence: Department of Public Administration, University of Kansas, 1987.

Nalbandian, J., and Edwards, J. T. "The Professional Values of Public Administrators: A Comparison with Lawyers, Social Workers, and Business Administrators." *Review of Public Personnel Administration*, 1983, *4*, 1-11.

Nathan, D. "Arlington City Manager Told to Decide on Cuts." *Dallas Morning News*, Mar. 8, 1989, p. 24A.

National Civic League. *Model City Charter*. (7th ed.) Denver: National Civic League, 1989.

National League of Cities. *A National Survey of City Council Members: Issues in Council Leadership*. Washington, D.C.: National League of Cities, 1980.

National Treasury Employees Union v. *William von Raab*. 57 LW 4338 (1989).

New York State Constitutional Convention Commission. *The Con-

stitution and Government of the State of New York. New York: Bureau of Municipal Research, 1915.

Newell, C., and Ammons, D. N. "Role Emphasis of City Managers and Other Municipal Executives." *Public Administration Review,* 1987, *47,* 246–253.

Newell, C., Glass, J. J., and Ammons, D. N. "City Manager Roles in a Changing Political Environment." In H. G. Frederickson (ed.), *Ideal and Practice in Council-Manager Government.* Washington, D.C.: International City Management Association, 1989.

Newland, C. A. "Council-Manager Government: Positive Alternative to Separation of Powers." *Public Management,* 1985, *67* (7), 7–9.

Newland, C. A. "The Future of Council-Manager Government." In H. G. Frederickson (ed.), *Ideal and Practice in Council-Manager Government.* Washington, D.C.: International City Management Association, 1989.

Olander, R. L. "Referendum Survival Techniques." *Public Management,* 1985, *67* (July), 11–13.

Perkins, J. Interviewed in J. Nalbandian and R. G. Davis (eds.), *Reflections of Local Government Professionals.* Lawrence: Department of Public Administration, University of Kansas, 1987.

Pickering v. *Board of Education,* 391 US 563 (1968).

Price, D. K. "The Promotion of the City Manager Plan." *Public Opinion Quarterly,* 1941, *5,* 563–578.

Price, D. K. *The Scientific Estate.* Cambridge, Mass.: Harvard University Press (Belknap Press), 1965.

Protasel, G. J. "Abandonments of the Council-Manager Plan: A New Institutional Perspective." *Public Administration Review,* 1988, *48* (July–Aug.), 807–812.

Protasel, G. J. "Leadership in Council-Manager Cities: The Institutional Implications." In H. G. Frederickson (ed.), *Ideal and Practice in Council-Manager Government.* Washington, D.C.: International City Management Association, 1989.

Ragland, J. "Minority Leaders Say They'll Take Alignment Fight to Court." *Dallas Morning News,* Apr. 26, 1990, p. 1A.

Redford, E. S. *Democracy in the Administrative State.* New York: Oxford University Press, 1969.

Reich, R. B. "Introduction." In R. B. Reich (ed.), *The Power of Public Ideas*. Cambridge, Mass.: Ballinger, 1988a.

Reich, R. B. "Policy Making in a Democracy." In R. B. Reich (ed.), *The Power of Public Ideas*. Cambridge, Mass.: Ballinger, 1988b.

Renner, T. *Municipal Election Processes: The Impact on Minority Representation*. Baseline Data Report, *19* (6). Washington, D.C.: International City Management Association, 1987.

Renner, T. *Elected Executives: Authority and Responsibility*. Baseline Data Report, *20* (3). Washington, D.C.: International City Management Association, 1988.

Ridley, C. E., and Nolting, O. *The City-Manager Profession*. Chicago: University of Chicago Press, 1934.

Rosenbloom, D. H. "Public Administration and the Judiciary: The 'New Partnership.'" *Public Administration Review*, 1987, *47*, 75–83.

Rosenbloom, D. H. "The Public Employment Relationship and the Supreme Court in the 1980s." *Review of Public Personnel Administration*, 1988, *48*, 49–65.

Rutter, L. *The Essential Community*. Washington, D.C.: International City Management Association, 1980.

Sanders, H. T. "The Government of American Cities: Continuity and Change in Structure." *Municipal Yearbook*. Washington, D.C.: International City Management Association, 1982.

Scheiber, W. Interviewed in J. Nalbandian and R. G. Davis (eds.), *Reflections of Local Government Professionals*. Lawrence: Department of Public Administration, University of Kansas, 1987.

Schellinger, M. A. *Today's Local Policy Makers: A Council Profile*. Baseline Data Report, *20* (4). Washington, D.C.: International City Management Association, 1988.

Schilling, E. G. "The Values of City Management." In H. G. Frederickson (ed.), *Ideal and Practice in Council-Manager Government*. Washington, D.C.: International City Management Association, 1989.

Schmidt, W. H., and Posner, B. Z. "Values and Expectations of City Managers in California." *Public Administration Review*, 1987, *47*, 404–409.

Schon, D. *Beyond the Stable State*. New York: Norton, 1973.

Scott, J. Interviewed in J. Nalbandian and R. G. Davis (eds.), *Re-*

flections of Local Government Professionals. Lawrence: Department of Public Administration, University of Kansas, 1987.

Seib, P. "City Charter Debate Includes Hidden Issues of Power." *Dallas Morning News,* Feb. 22, 1989, p. 19A.

Sharp, E. B. *Citizen Demand-making in the Urban Context.* University, Ala.: University of Alabama Press, 1986.

Sharp, E. B. "City Management in an Era of Blurred Boundaries." In H. G. Frederickson (ed.), *Ideal and Practice in Council-Manager Government.* Washington, D.C.: International City Management Association, 1989.

Sharpe, C. F. "Reflections on Leaving the Public Service." *Public Administration Review,* 1969, *29,* 403–409.

Simon, H. A. *Administrative Behavior.* (3rd ed.) New York: Free Press, 1945, reissued 1976.

Skinner v. *Railway Labor Executives' Association,* 57 LW 4323 (1989).

Sparrow, G. "The Emerging Chief Executive: The San Diego Experience." *National Civic Review,* 1985, *74* (Dec.), 538–547.

Stillman II, R. J. *The Rise of the City Manager.* Albuquerque: University of New Mexico Press, 1974.

Stillman II, R. J. "The City Manager: Professional Helping Hand, or Political Hired Hand?" *Public Administration Review,* 1977, *37* (6), 659–670.

Stillman II, R. J. "Local Public Management in Transition: A Report on the Current State of the Profession." *Municipal Yearbook.* Washington, D.C.: International City Management Association, 1982.

Stone, H. A., Price, D. K., and Stone, K. H. *City Manager Government in the United States: A Review After Twenty-Five Years.* Chicago: Public Administration Service, 1940.

Strauss Pealy, D. "The Need for Elected Leadership." *Public Administration Review,* 1958, *18* (Summer), 214–216.

Streib, G. "Professionalism and Support for Democratic Principles: The Case of Local Government Department Heads in Northern Illinois." Unpublished manuscript, School of Public Administration and Urban Studies, Georgia State University, Atlanta, 1990.

Svara, J. H. "Dichotomy and Duality: Reconceptualizing the Relationship Between Policy and Administration in Council-Manager Cities." *Public Administration Review*, 1985, *45*, 221–232.

Svara, J. H. "The Complementary Roles of Officials in Council-Manager Government." *Municipal Yearbook*. Washington, D.C.: International City Management Association, 1988.

Svara, J. H. "Is There a Future for City Managers? The Evolving Roles of Officials in Council-Manager Government." *International Journal of Public Administration*, 1989a, *12*, 179–212.

Svara, J. H. "Mayors and City Managers in the 1990s: Allies or Antagonists." Paper presented at the 1989 meeting of the American Society for Public Administration, Miami, Apr. 9, 1989b.

Svara, J. H. "Policy and Administration: City Managers As Comprehensive Professional Leaders." In H. G. Frederickson (ed.), *Ideal and Practice in Council-Manager Government*. Washington, D.C.: International City Management Association, 1989c.

Svara, J. H. "Progressive Roots of the Model Charter and the Manager Profession: A Positive Heritage." *National Civic Review*, 1989d, *78* (5), 339–355.

Svara, J. H. *Official Leadership in the City: Patterns of Conflict and Cooperation*. New York: Oxford University Press, 1990.

"The Svehla Appointment." *Kansas City Times*, June 9, 1989, p. A-12.

Thomas, J. C. *Between Citizen and City*. Lawrence: University Press of Kansas, 1986.

Thomas, J. C. "Public Involvement in Public Management: Adapting and Testing a Borrowed Theory." *Public Administration Review*, 1990, *50*, 435–445.

Thompson, J. D. *Organizations in Action*. New York: McGraw-Hill, 1967.

Thornburg v. *Gingles*, 106 S.Ct. 2752 (1986).

Tipton, H. D. "Response to 'Nature of City Managers' Work.'" In H. G. Frederickson (ed.), *Ideal and Practice in Council-Manager Government*. Washington, D.C.: International City Management Association, 1989.

Urwick, L. "Organization As a Technical Problem." In L. Gulick and L. Urwick (eds.), *Papers on the Science of Administration*. New York: Institute of Public Administration, 1937a.

Urwick, L. "The Function of Administration." In L. Gulick and L. Urwick (eds.), *Papers on the Science of Administration*. New York: Institute of Public Administration, 1937b.

Valdez, J. Interviewed in J. Nalbandian and R. G. Davis (eds.), *Reflections of Local Government Professionals*. Lawrence: Department of Public Administration, University of Kansas, 1987.

Waldo, D. *The Administrative State: A Study of the Political Theory of American Public Administration*. New York: Ronald Press, 1948. Reissued (2nd ed.) New York: Holmes and Meier, 1984.

Wamsley, G. L., and others. "The Public Administration and the Governance Process: Refocusing the American Dialogue." In R. C. Chandler (ed.), *A Centennial History of the American Administrative State*. New York: Free Press, 1987.

Watkins, D. F. Interviewed by E. Leonard III. Department of Public Administration, University of Kansas, Lawrence, Apr. 20, 1986.

Watkins, D. F. "Response to 'The Future of Council-Manager Government'." In H. G. Frederickson (ed.), *Ideal and Practice in Council-Manager Government*. Washington, D.C.: International City Management Association, 1989.

Watson v. Fort Worth Bank and Trust. 108 S.Ct. 2777 (1988).

White, L. D. *Introduction to the Study of Public Administration*. New York: Macmillan, 1926.

White, L. D. *The City Manager*. Chicago: University of Chicago Press, 1927.

Wikstrom, N. "The Mayor As a Policy Leader in the Council-Manager Form of Government: A View from the Field." *Public Administration Review*, 1979, *39*, 270–276.

Willbern, Y. "Types and Levels of Public Morality." *Public Administration Review*, 1984, *44*, 10–21.

Willoughby, W. F. *Principles of Public Administration*. Washington, D.C.: The Brookings Institution, 1927.

Wilson, W. "The Study of Administration." *Political Science Quarterly*, 1887. Reprinted in J. M. Shafritz and A. C. Hyde (eds.), *Classics of Public Administration*. Chicago: Dorsey, 1987.

Yates, D. *The Ungovernable City*. Cambridge, Mass.: MIT Press, 1977.

Index

A

Aberbach, J. D., 78
Abilene, Texas, educational role in, 101
Abney, G., 24, 25
Accountability: and administrative power, 22-28; aspects of, 69-84; background on, 69-71; behind the scenes, 74-75; conclusions on, 83-84; and council authority, 73-74; political, and administrative neutrality, 9-12; and political leadership, 28-31; and political nature of problem solving, 78-83; in practice, 72-78; traditions of, 71-72
Ackoff, R. L., 78
Administration: and accountability, 22-28; city managers in charge of, 59; council involvement in, 28; neutrality of, 9-12, 22-24; politics isolated from, 5-9, 107-108; role of politics in, 63-66
Adrian, C. R., 29, 37, 47, 51
Ammons, D. N., 4, 42, 53, 56, 57n
Anderson, C., 77, 78, 98
Anderson, E. A., 47, 51, 76, 78
Appleby, P., 19
Arizona. See Tucson
Arkansas City, Kansas, efficiency value in, 88
Arlington, Texas, and accountability, 75

Arlington County, Virginia, and accountability, 75-76
Ashburner, C. E., 72
At-large elections, of council, 32-35. See also Representation
Authority, policy-making, 73-74
Azevedo, L., 34-35

B

Banfield, E. C., 29, 32
Banovetz, J. M., 40
Barnett, C., 81-82
Barrett, R. A., 20
Barta, C., 34
Beer, M., 82-83
Bellah, R. N., 71, 94, 98, 99
Blackmun, H., 93
Blagg, J., 101
Blubaugh, D. A., 88
Bollens, J. C., 53, 87
Bonsey, O., 29, 100, 101
Booth, D. A., 37, 38-39
Bosworth, K. A., 4
Boynton, R. P., 37, 38
Branscome, C., 73, 94-95
Bromage, A. W., 4
Brown, L. J., 75-76, 77-78
Buchmeyer, J., 40, 46
Burns, J. M., 20

C

Cabanatuan, M., 48
California: council-manager form

124

Index

59. *See also* Concord; Ingle-
wood; Long Beach; Los Angeles
County; Oxnard; Palm Springs;
San Diego; Santa Ana; Walnut
Creek
Carman, B., 26-27
Chamber of Commerce, and representation, 35
Charter reform, in Dallas, 43-47
Childs, R. S., 9, 11, 15, 37
Cincinnati, neighborhood groups
in, 21, 63
Cisneros, H., 94
Citizenship: participative role of,
63-66; reflective, 104
City managers: and administration,
59; behind-the-scenes work of,
74-75; calling for, 71-72; council
guidance for, 75-76; as educator
in values, 99-102; expectations
for, 57-58; as general managers,
15; policy making by, 56-59, 99;
and policy-making void, 58-59,
75-76; political involvement of,
53-62; as power brokers, 56-62;
power of, 24-26; problem solving by, 76-83, 101; as prototype,
108; responsibilities of, 69-84;
roles of, 10-11, 51-68; successful,
105-106; transformations for,
103-104; and values, 85-102. *See
also* Council-manager
government
City Managers' Association, 15, 72
Coile, N., 24, 25
Colorado. *See* Fort Collins
Concord, California: professional
politicians in, 21; representation
in, 34-35
Connolly, W., 32
Constitution: First Amendment to,
92; Fourth Amendment to, 65,
92
Cooper, T. L., 70
Council: administrative involvement of, 28; at-large election of,
32-35; authority from, for policy
making, 73-74; and expectations

of manager, 57-58; guidance
from, 75-76; and independent
information, 27-28; and professional staff, 26-27
Council-manager government: accountability and neutrality in,
9-12; adaptive responses in, 36-
48; administrative power and accountability in, 22-28; aspects
of, 3-18; assumptions of, 107-
108; background on, 3-5; challenges to, 19-35; charter reform
for, 43-47; conclusions on, 17-
18, 35; contemporary political
environments for, 20-22; for efficiency and community har-
mony, 16-17; for efficiency and
public interest, 13-15; goals of,
19; legitimacy of, 47-48, 69-84;
partnership model of, 67-68;
political leadership and accountability in, 28-31; politics-
administration dichotomy in, 5-
9, 107-108; professionalism in,
42-43; representation in, 32-35,
39-41; roles in, 51-68. *See also*
City managers
Crane, R. T., 6, 13
Crawford, S., 27

D

Dallas: and accountability, 77, 81;
and administrative neutrality,
23; charter reform in, 33, 43-47;
council-manager form in, 48;
political diversity in, 21, 60, 66;
professional staff in, 27-28; representation in, 33-34, 40, 44-45,
90, 98; social equity in, 94
Davis, R. G., 66
Dayton, charter of, 10
Daytona Beach: and educational
role, 100; manager's activities in,
55
Decatur, Georgia, and accountability, 73
Delaware, Ohio, special interests
in, 22

Democracy, values of, 89–95
Dever, J., 59, 107
District of Columbia: and accountability, 72; and cooperation, 54
Diversity, political, 20–21
Downs, T., 72, 91
Drug testing, and individual rights, 65–66

E

Eau Claire, Wisconsin, and accountability, 76
Education, in values by managers, 99–102
Edwards, J. T., 59, 71
Efficiency: and community harmony, 16–17; and public interest, 13–15; as value, 86–89, 97
Ehrenhalt, A., 21, 34–35, 70, 81–82
Eisenstat, R. A., 82–83
Emery, F. E., 104
Equity, social, 92–95, 97
Eugene, Oregon, public committees in, 64–65

F

Fayol, H., 14
Fitzpatrick, J. C., 28
Florida, mayors elected in, 37. *See also* Daytona Beach; Hillsborough County
Flournoy, C., 27
Foell, D., 29
Fort Collins, Colorado, and political leadership, 30–31
Fort Worth: and accountability, 74; diversity in, 66
Frederickson, H. G., 94
Freeland, C., 88
Friedrich, C. J., 32, 100
Funkhouser, M., 28

G

Gaebler, T., 30, 100
Georgia. *See* Decatur
Germany, and efficiency, 13

Glass, J. J., 42
Gleason, M., 63–65
Goodnow, F. J., 6, 8, 9
Gottdiener, M., 32, 90
Green, R. E., 25, 53, 57, 61, 78
Gresham, Oregon, professional staff in, 26–27
Griesemer, J. R., 55, 82, 88–89
Gruber, J. E., 27, 68, 71, 80
Gulick, L., 15, 16

H

Haber, S., 13, 16, 32
Hale, M. L., 53, 60, 61, 62n, 76, 100
Hall-Saltzstein, G., 71, 96
Hansell, W., 95
Harmon, B. D., 20
Hart, J., 81
Hays, S. P., 32
Herchert, R., 74
Hero, R. E., 92
Hickey, N., 22
Hillsborough County, Florida: and accountability, 75–76, 77; professional politicians in, 22
Hinton, D. W., 53, 60
Hofstadter, R., 32
Housewright, E., 21, 27, 34
Huntley, R. J., 57, 58n

I

Illinois, representation in, 91
Individual rights: and drug testing, 65–66; as value, 91–92, 97
Information, independent, for council, 27–28
Inglewood, California, individual rights in, 92
International City Management Association (ICMA), 11, 21, 41, 43, 54, 73, 74, 79, 101, 105; Code of Ethics of, 7, 12, 47, 74, 85, 95; Declaration of Ideals of, 47, 93, 95; Future Horizons for, 4, 60, 104; surveys by, 20, 25, 57, 59, 61–62, 71, 78

International Personnel Management Association, 74

J

Jackson, D., 94
Jennings, B., 83
Johnson County, Kansas, efficiency
value in, 88

K

Kahn, R. L., 55
Kammerer, G., 37
Kansas. *See* Arkansas City; Johnson
County; Lawrence; Lenexa;
Olathe
Kansas City, Missouri: and ac-
countability, 74; and administra-
tive neutrality, 23; city
management in, 48; diversity in,
66; and independent informa-
tion, 28; neighborhood groups
in, 21, 63; and representation, 35
Katz, D., 55
Kaufman, H., 43, 100
Keane, M., 54
Kelley, C., 33-34
Kerner Commission, 40
Kerrigan, J. E., 53, 60
King, N. R., 87
Kipp, R., 21, 29, 72, 74
Kirchoff, W., 55, 75, 82, 99
Kirkpatrick, S., 30-31
Knight, City Manager, 27
Krislov, S., 24

L

Lane, L. M., 70
Lauth, T. P., 24, 25
Lawrence, Kansas: and account-
ability, 80-81; representation in,
32-33; values trade-offs in, 96-98
Leadership, political, 28-31, 36-39,
43-44
League of California Municipali-
ties, 48
Legitimacy: and accountability, 69-

84; of council-manager form,
47-48
Leiker, V., 28
Lenexa, Kansas, and city manager
power, 25-26
Lesser, P., 33-34
Lewinsohn, T., 74-75
Lipscomb, A., 33-34
Lipset, S. M., 32
Local government: adaptive responses in, 36-48; challenges to,
19-35; contemporary professionalism in, 49-108; council-
manager form of, 3-18; evolution of design for, 1-48; structural reforms of, 105
Long Beach, California, and manager's motivation, 59, 107
Los Angeles County: manager's activities in, 61-62; representation
in, 90
Lowi, T. J., 68
Lukas, A. J., 29-30

M

McClelland, D., 106
McClure, W., 48
Macdonald, R. J., 57, 58n
McIntire, D., 26
MacIntyre, A., 106-107
Maine. *See* Yarmouth
Managers. *See* City managers
Manahan, J., 88
March, J. G., 107
Margolis, S., 92
Martinez, R., 21
Mayors: direct election of, 36-39;
role of, 38
Metropolitan Washington Council
of Governments, 54
Miller, Council Member, 25
Minkin, P., 32
Minorities. *See* Representation
Missouri. *See* Kansas City
Mooney, J. D., 16
Mora, D., 73
Mosher, F. C., 68

Mulrooney, K. F., 40
Murray, S., 79–80, 91, 95

N

Nalbandian, J., 59, 62*n*, 66, 71, 92
Nathan, D., 75
National Civic League, Model City
    Charter of, 10–11, 40
*National Treasury Employees
    Union* v. *William von Raab*, 65,
    92
National League of Cities, 20, 58
Neutrality: of administration, 9–12,
    22–24; concepts of, 11–12
New Jersey, diversity in, 91
New York. *See* Yonkers
New York State Constitutional
    Convention Commission, 10
Newell, C., 4, 42, 53, 56, 57*n*
Newland, C. A., 20, 66
Nolting, O., 8, 10, 11–12
North Carolina: mayors elected in,
    37; policy making in, 56–57, 67;
    representation in, 40

O

Ohio: involvement in, 67; mayors
    elected in, 37. *See also* Cincin-
    nati; Dayton; Delaware; Toledo
Olander, R. L., 43
Olathe, Kansas, representation in,
    35
Olsen, J., 107
Olson, D., 23
Oregon. *See* Eugene; Gresham
Organization: as machine, 16; as
    social construction, 106
Oxnard, California, and account-
    ability, 73

P

Palm Springs, California, effi-
    ciency value in, 87
Paul, D., 27
Perkins, J., 90–91
Pickering v. *Board of Education*, 92
Policy making: behind the scenes,

74–75; by city managers, 56–59,
    99; council authority for, 73–74;
    expectations on, 57–58; impor-
    tance of, 56–58; as problem solv-
    ing, 76–78, 106–107; process and
    substance in, 99; void in, 58–59,
    75–76
Political leadership: and account-
    ability, 28–31; adaptations in,
    36–39; increasing, 43–44
Political machines, role of, 6
Politics: accountability in, 9–12;
    administration isolated from, 5–
    9, 107–108; city managers' in-
    volvement in, 53–62; contempo-
    rary environment of, 20–22;
    diversity in, 20–21; and problem
    solving, 78–83; professionalism
    in, and special interests, 21–22;
    role of, in administration, 63–66;
    transactional and transforma-
    tional, 20
Posner, B. Z., 62
Power: administrative, and ac-
    countability, 22–28; brokering,
    by city manager, 56–62; of city
    managers, 24–26
Price, D. K., 3, 4, 11, 12, 15, 17, 24,
    53
Problem solving: policy making as,
    76–78, 106–107; political nature
    of, 78–73
Professionalism: and accountabil-
    ity, 69–84; adaptations in, 42–43;
    aspects of contemporary, 49–108;
    and democracy, 89–95; and effi-
    ciency, 86–89; future of, 103–108;
    maintaining, 45; in politics, 21–
    22; roles in, 51–68; tenets of, 52–
    53; value base of, 85–105; virtues
    of, 106–107
Progressive movement, 17
Protasel, G. J., 30, 39
Putnam, R. D., 78

R

Ragland, J., 46
Ragsdale, D., 28, 33–34

Redford, E. S., 68, 89
Reich, R. B., 100, 101, 102
Reiley, A., 16
Renner, T., 40-41, 51, 105
Representation: adaptations for,
    39-41; in council-manager form,
    32-35, 39-41; increasing minor-
    ity, 44-45; as value, 90-91, 96, 97
Responsibility: and accountability,
    69-84; and professionalism, 52,
    70
Responsiveness: and value trade-
    offs, 95-98; values in, 86
Ridley, C. E., 8, 10, 11-12
Ries, J. C., 53, 87
Rights, individual, 65-66, 91-92, 97
Rockman, B. A., 78
Roles: aspects of contemporary, 51-
    68; background on, 51-53; of
    city manager in politics, 53-62;
    conclusions on, 66-68; of policy
    making, 56-59; of politics in ad-
    ministration, 63-66; and profes-
    sionalism, 52
Rosenbloom, D. H., 24, 65, 66, 92
Rucker, J., 27
Rutter, L., 53, 60

S

San Diego: and accountability, 79-
    80; diversity in, 66; and represen-
    tation, 91
Sanders, H. T., 30, 42
Santa Ana, California, and repre-
    sentation, 90
Scheiber, W., 54
Schellinger, M. A., 41
Schilling, E. G., 59, 67
Schmidt, W. H., 62
Schon, D., 104
Schrader, G., 60
Scientific management movement,
    14-15
Scott, J., 22, 26
Seib, P., 23
Sharp, E. B., 20, 21, 63
Sharpe, C. F., 73
Shields, Council Member, 28

Short ballot movement, 9-10
Simon, H. A., 19, 89, 101
Skinner v. Railway Labor Execu-
    tives' Association, 92
Social equity, as value, 92-95, 97
Sparrow, G., 29
Special interests, and professional
    politicians, 21-22
Spector, B., 82-83
Staff, professional: adaptations by,
    42-43; distrust of, 26-27; main-
    taining professionalism of, 45
Stene, J., 59-60
Stillman, R. J., II, 3-4, 7, 12, 15, 17,
    53, 62, 78, 82, 99
Stone, H. A., 4, 11, 12, 15, 17, 53
Stone, K. H., 4, 11, 12, 15, 17, 53
Strauss, A., 21
Strauss Pealy, D., 29
Streib, G., 39, 65, 91
Svara, J. H., 3, 4, 7, 10, 12, 16, 24,
    28, 29, 37, 38, 53, 56-57, 58, 62,
    66, 67, 75, 100, 101

T

Tandy, C., 27, 94
Taylor, F. W., 14
Teamsters v. United States, 93
Texas. See Abilene; Arlington; Dal-
    las; Fort Worth
Thomas, J. C., 21, 63, 89
Thompson, J. D., 89
Thornburg v. Gingles, 39-40
Tipton, H. D., 55, 56, 75, 100
Toledo, Ohio, and political leader-
    ship, 30, 31
Trist, E. L., 104
Tucson: city manager power in, 24,
    25; social equity in, 93-94

U

U.S. Customs Service, and drug
    testing, 65
U.S. District Court, and representa-
    tion, 40, 45, 46
U.S. Supreme Court: and at-large

elections, 39–40; and drug testing, 65; and social equity, 93
Urwick, L., 14, 16

V

Valdez, J., 24, 25, 93–94
Values: aspects of, 85–102; background on, 85–86; conclusions on, 102; of democracy, 89–95; education in, 99–102; of efficiency, 86–89, 97; implications of, 95–102; of individual rights, 91–92, 97; and policy-making process and substance, 99; and professionalism, 52–53, 85–102, 104–105; of representation, 90–91, 96, 97; of social equity, 92–95, 97; trade-offs of, 95–98
Virginia, mayors in, 38. *See also* Arlington County
Virtues, of professionalism, 106–107
Voting Rights Act of 1963, 90
Voting Rights Act of 1965, 40

W

Waite, H. M., 9
Waldo, D., 9, 13, 14, 19

Walnut Creek, California, efficiency value in, 88
Wamsley, G. L., 70, 79
Washington, D. C.: and accountability, 72; and cooperation, 54
Watkins, D. F., 25–26, 35
Watson v. *Fort Worth Bank and Trust*, 93
Wedel, K., 59
Weiss, J., 34
Wheeler, Council Member, 25
White, L. D., 4, 8, 10, 11, 12, 14, 17, 29
Wikstrom, N., 38
Wildgen, M., 80–81
Willbern, Y., 79
Willoughby, W. F., 14, 15, 16
Wilson, J. Q., 29, 32
Wilson, W., 7–8
Wisconsin. *See* Eau Claire
Wolf, J. F., 70
Wright, D. S., 37, 38, 56, 57n

Y

Yarmouth, Maine, educational role in, 101
Yates, D., 22
Yonkers, and political leadership, 29–30